PLANNING AND MANAGEMENT OF SCIENCE INFORMATION SYSTEMS

PLANNING AND MANAGEMENT OF SCIENCE INFORMATION SYSTEMS

Prof. C.A. Augustine

Ess Ess Publications
New Delhi

PLANNING AND MANAGEMENT OF SCIENCE INFORMATION SYSTEMS

ISBN : 978-81-947398-6-9

Price : Rs. 950/-

First Published 2021

Published by:
Ess Ess Publications
4831/24, Ansari Road,
Darya Ganj,
New Delhi-110 002.
INDIA
Phones: 23260807, 41563444
Fax: 41563334
E-mail: info@essessreference.com
www.essessreference.com

Cover Design by Patch Creative Unit

Printed and bound in India

Contents

Preface

An information System is a deliberate arrangement made for the storage and retrieval of information by collecting, organizing, and making accessible the records of all relevant information to those who need them. It is an organized combination of people, hardware, software, communication networks and data resources that collect, transform and disseminate information in an organization. Now-a-days all kinds of organizations, industrial companies, government establishments, business firms, and R & D institutions have been giving increasing attention to the design and development of information systems to meet their complex information needs. These Science Information Systems may be known by different names like special libraries, information centres, information analysis centres, information retrieval systems, etc. Irrespective of the difference in names their overall purpose and function are similar. Nevertheless, their meticulous planning and management are crucially important. This book is an exercise in this direction. As such, it is intended to meet the requirement of teachers and students of the M.L.I.Sc degree courses in respect of their optional paper on Science Information Systems Management. The text is organized into 10 chapters, each of which is on a major area of the subject. Chapter 1 is An Introduction to Management where the concept of management is examined from different perspectives like a science, a profession, principles of scientific management and strategic management. Chapter 2 examines the concepts of Science and Science Information Systems. Chapter 3 is a detailed study of the Science and Technology set up in India. Chapter 4 is on Planning of Science Information Systems. Chapters 5 to 9 are devoted to subjects, like User Community and its Requirements, Collection Development and Management, Information Products and Services, Human Resources Planning, and Financial Planning and Budgeting. Finally, Chapter 10 discusses Evaluation of Library and Information Systems. For many years I have been teaching these subjects, but the present text has been updated recently. I hope, that the book will serve as a dependable tool for both students and teachers alike.

I would like to place on record my sincere gratitude to Mr. Sumit Sethi of M/s Ess Ess Publications, New Delhi, for accepting this book for publishing.

— Prof. C.A. Augustine

Trivandrum,
01 January 2021

The Book

This book, *Planning and Management of Science Information Systems* comes out with 10 chapters each of which dealing with a significant area in the subject at large, like: Introduction to Management, Science Information Systems, Science and Technology Set up in India, Planning of Science Information systems, User Community and its Requirements, Collect ion Development and Management, Information Products and Services, Human Resources Planning, Financial Planning and Budgeting, and Evaluation of Library and Information Systems. There is also a Bibliography attached at the end.

The Author

Prof. C. A. Augustine having retired from the University of Kerala as Head of the Department of Library & Information Science in 1991 served in the Kerala Agricultural University as its Professor & Library Advisor until August 1995. During this period he was responsible for planning and designing the Central University Library Building for the Kerala Agricultural University at Vellanikkara, Thrissur, and for developing other library buildings in distant university campuses like Vellayani, and. for proposing the **Kerala Agricultural University Library and Information System & Computer Network (KAULIS & LISNET)**. Since then he has been working as Guest Faculty in different universities and he has been the grand teacher of more than 5 generations of library science teachers. His long experience in teaching and the profession has led to his enormous contributions in library and information science literature with several books and compilations including about 100 learned papers. His latest book, *Information Science: Information, Knowledge, Communication and Libraries* (2021) has been well received by the professional community.

1
An Introduction to Management

'Management' is at present a subject of specialization where systematic education, training and practical experience are necessary in order to qualify any one for a management position, in either business, industry, government or public administration, charitable societies or welfare organizations. There are many a definitions for 'management'.

Many management thinkers have defined management in their own ways. According to F.W. Taylor (1909) "*management is an art ofknowing what to do when to do and see that it is done in the best and cheapest way*". Henri Fayol (1916), the father of scientific management, had defined it "*as the process of forecasting, planning, organizing, commanding, coordinating, and controlling*". According to *Business Dictionary*, management is '*the organization and coordination of the activities of a business in order to achieve defined objectives (www.businessdictionary.com)*. According to another source, "*Management is a process or an activity that brings together several varied resources like persons, materials, techniques, and technologies to accomplish a task or tasks*" (IGNOU, 1989). Nevertheless, management is generally understood as partly, the process of getting things done through people, and partly, the creative and energetic combination of scarce resources into effective and profitable activities, and the combination of the skills and talents of the individuals concerned with doing this. Management is a set of principles relating to the functions of planning, organizing, directing and controlling, and the application of these principles in harnessing physical, financial, human, and informational resources efficiently and effectively to achieve organizational goals.

MANAGEMENT AS A SCIENCE

Modern management is characterized by a scientific approach which involves, mainly 6 aspects:

(1) Application of scientific methods and scientific analysis to managerial functions and problems;

(2) Emphasis on the human elements in management, based on various psychological studies and behavioural analysis in specific situations;

(3) Increasing thrust on economic effectives in all management functions;

(4) A system approach, focusing equal attention on all functions of management;

(5) Use of electronic computers for analysis and studies; and

(6) Application of automation through the involvement of Information and Communication Technology.

The different areas in management where scientific methods are found applied are mainly in:

- Contributions from disciplines such as mathematics, statistics and economics;
- Mathematical models for planning, decision making and forecasting;
- Operations research studies for operational efficiency,
- Economic analysis for cost-benefit and cost-effectiveness studies;

- Theories of leadership and organization, human behaviour and motivation;
- Systems approach.

As a science there are precise elements, scientific and exact aspects that have to be learned and assimilated in management. For example, a good grasp of certain quantitative methods and financial and statistical data, as well as certain, less scientific but well tried and tested elements such as human motivation, and the effect of different payment systems on the performance of different expectations.

MANAGEMENT AS A PROFESSION

Management is now more and more recognized as a profession. A profession may be defined as an occupation that requires specialized knowledge and intensive academic preparations to which entry is regulated by a representative body. Management is variously described as a science, a profession, and an art. But the truth of its status lies somewhere between the three, and that the subject has strong elements of all the three. As a science, there are precise elements, scientific and exact aspects that have to be learned and assimilated. For example, a good grasp of certain quantitative methods and financial and statistical data, as well as certain, less scientific but well tried and tested, elements such as human motivation, the effect of different payment systems and expectations on performance, etc. As a profession, in so far as there is a general recognition, there are certain knowledge, skills and aptitudes that must be assimilated and understood by any one who aspires to be a truly effective manager. Management is an art in the sense that within some constraints and strictures there is great scope for the use of creativity, imagination, initiative and innovation within the overall sphere of the occupation. Knowledge referred to already must be applied in their own way to each and any given situation, issue or problem. This is the creative aspect of the manager's role and function, and anyone in a managerial position who seeks for prescriptive solutions to organization's problems is likely to fail. Although the subject of management may appear to be both precise and vague at the same time, it is possible to pin down certain elements that are present in all effective management and successful managers, the most critical of these elements are **communication** and **decision making**. Anyone who aspires to management must understand the processes involved in both these and must be able to carry them out effectively in specific situations. The abilities in communication and decision making are fundamental to the success of any managerial activity

The overall management task is concerned with:

- getting things done through people;
- the combination and ordering of a variety of resources for given productive purposes;
- the balancing of resource utilization with the commercial, environmental and operational variables of quantity, quality and time; and
- coping with change and uncertainty.

Management although is at the same time an art, science and profession has emerged as a distinct field of study out of years of experience acquired mainly in business and industry.

SCIENTIFIC MANAGEMENT

The concept of scientific management was originally introduced in 1911 by Frederick Winslow Taylor through his famous monograph under the title '*The principles of scientific management*'. Because of the seminal nature of the ideas contained in this text, he came to be called in later years as 'The Father of Scientific Management" and his approach is referred to as 'Taylor's Principles' or 'Taylorism'. Taylor was a mechanical engineer and a manager in an American manufacturing company. His major concern was about the 'wasted human efforts' due mainly to an attitude of workers called 'soldiering', meaning the deliberate slowing down of work to protect their class interests since they wrongly believed that by doing more work they will be making more workmen jobless. Taylor asserted that this inefficiency of workmen could be overcome by training and development of individual workers. The remedy lies in systematic management rather than searching for an unusual or extraordinary worker. According to Taylor, the best management is a true science resting upon clearly defined laws, rules and principles as a foundation. The fundamental principles of scientific management are applicable to all kinds of human activities, from the simple acts of an individual to the very complex corporate activities. Taylor's famous Principles of Scientific Management consisted of 4 principles and they may be stated here as follows:

(1) Management is to develop a science for each element of a man's work, to replace the old rule-of-thump method;

(2) Management is responsible for the scientific selection of workmen and their training, teaching and development where as in the past the worker was choosing his own work and training himself as best as he could;

(3) Management is to heartily co-operate with the men so as to insure all, of the work being done in accordance with the principles of the science which has been developed; and

(4) There is an almost equal division of the work and the responsibility between the management and the workmen. . The management takes over all work for which they are better fitted than the workmen, while in the past all of the work and the greater part of the responsibility were thrown upon the workmen

According to F.W. Taylor "*scientific management implies the application of the following two fold techniques: 1. The discovery of the best method of performing a particular work; 2. The best method or fruitful method for meeting a given situation... Scientific management will be that kind of a process of directing human efforts. Scientific management means knowing exactly what you want men to do and seeing that they do it in the best and the cheapest way".*

Scientific management is a theory of management that analyzes and synthesizes workflows with the main objective of improving economic efficiency, especially labour productivity. Frederick Winslow Taylor (1909) who started the scientific management movement proposed that by optimizing and simplifying jobs, productivity would increase. He advanced the idea that workers and managers needed to cooperate with one another and by studying the work process scientifically, that work can be performed in relation to worker productivity. Taylor believed that workers were motivated by money and so he promoted the idea of "a fair day's pay for a fair day's work". Taylor's 4 Principles of Scientific Management known simply as "Taylorism" can be stated as follows:

(1) Replace working by rule of thump and instead use the scientific method to study work and determine the most efficient way to perform specific tasks;

(2) Rather than simply assign workers to just any job, match workers to their jobs based on capability and motivation, and train them to work at maximum efficiency;

(3) Monitor worker performance, and provide instructions and supervision to ensure that they are using the most efficient ways of working; and

(4) Allocate the work between managers and workers so that the managers spend their time planning and training, allowing the workers to perform their tasks efficiently.

Peter Drucker (1973) saw Fredrick Taylor as the creator of knowledge management, because the aim of scientific management was to produce knowledge about how to improve work processes. Although the typical application of scientific management was in manufacturing, Taylor himself advocated scientific management for all sorts of work, including the management of universities and government.

FAYOL'S PRINCIPLES OF MANAGEMENT

Almost 5 years later, Henri Fayol came out with his Principles of Management (*General and industrial administration,* 1916). Fayol belonged to the Administrative Management school of thought as opposed to the Scientific Management school, led by Frederick Taylor.

Fayol identified **6 Primary Functions of Management,** namely:

(1) Forecasting,

(2) Planning,

(3) Organizing,

(4) Commanding,

(5) Coordinating, and

(6) Controlling.

He also evolved **14 Management Principles**. These principles are listed and briefly introduced below for your knowledge:

1. Division of Work : Work should be divided among individuals and groups to ensure that efforts and attention are focused on special portions of a task. This leads to work specialization, and in turn, greater efficiency, ease of control, and increased output.

2. Authority : Managers must have the authority to give orders, but they must also keep in mind that with authority comes responsibility also. Responsibility involves being accountable.

3. Discipline : *A successful organization requires the* *common effort of workers and this is the discipline that should be encouraged and enforced under penalty. Discipline* encompasses regularity, behaviour, conduct, accountability, interpersonal relationship, and other essential qualities of the staff;

4. Unity of Command : Each employee has an identified and recognized superior or commander, i.e. he receives orders from only one manager.

5. Unity of Direction : The entire organization should be moving towards a common objective in a common direction. Teams with the same objective have to work under the direction of one manager, using one plan. This will ensure that all actions are properly coordinated.

6. Subordination : Individual interests must be only subordinate to the general interests of the organization. The interests of one person should not be allowed to become more important than those of the group. This includes also managers.

7. Remuneration : Remuneration and reward must be in a fair and equitable manner to all, because employee satisfaction depends very much on this factor.

8. Centralization : There must be centrality of control, but at the same time, the employees should be kept closer to the decision making process.

9. Scalar Chain : There must be a Top-to-Bottom Line of Authority which is discernible. Employees should be aware of where they stand in the hierarchy or chain of command. Lower level managers should always keep upper level managers informed of their work and activities. The scalar chain and its adherence are necessary for any organization to be successful..

10. Order : Order must be the hall mark of an organization. This involves the clean and tidy workplace facilities, the safety of employees, and the coordination of materials and people in specific activities;.

11. Equity : The principle of dealing fairly with everybody who works for the organization. This will ensure that everybody receives the same standard of treatment in the organization.

12. Stability : Stability of Job Tenure must be there by which all employees will stand to get continuity of employment. This will be in the interests of building up the expertise of the organization also.

13. Initiative : There must be proper encouragement of Initiatives of everyone who works in the organization through incentives and rewards so as to stimulate original thinking, innovation in work, and performance quality.

14. Espirit De Corps : Management should encourage generating in the managers and the employees an organizational culture (corporate culture), team spirit, and group identity. (*https://www.managementstudying.com downloaded on 20/07/2020*).

Fayol's 14 Principles of Management have been a significant influence on modern management theory. His practical list of principles helped early 20th century managers learn how to organize and interact with their employees in a productive way. Although the 14 Principles aren't widely used today, they can still offer guidance for today's managers. (*www.mindtools.com downloaded on 20/07/2020*). Many of the principles are now considered to be common sense, but at the time of their publication they were revolutionary concepts for organizational management.

POSDCORB FORMULA OF MANAGEMENT

Management can be viewed as a set of common processes or functions which, when carried out correctly, lead to organizational efficiency and effectiveness. These functional elements are interrelated and interdependent. Analyzing and identifying them will help in streamlining the total administration for greater efficiency. In 1937, two authors, Luther Gulick and Lyndal Urwick through their joint paper on '*Administrative management theory*' accomplished a systematic analysis of a manager's job. (*www.BusinessDictionary.com*). They introduced what later came to be known as the POSDCORB formula. POSDCORB is an acronym representing the 7 functional responsibilities of a Chief Executive Officer as formulated by them, namely

- Planning,
- Organizing,
- Staffing,
- Directing,
- Coordinating,
- Reporting, and
- Budgeting

POSDCORB is an acronym that has been widely used in the field of management and public administration that reflects the classic view of organizational theory. These elements need be explained in detail:

Planning : Planning is creating a plan of action for the future determining the stages of the plan and the technology necessary to implement it. Planning enables deciding in advance what to do, how to do it, when to do it and who should do it. It maps the path from where the organization is to where it wants to be. The planning function involves establishing goals and arranging them in a logical order.

Organizing : Once a plan of action is designed, managers need to provide everything necessary to carry it out, including raw materials, tools, capital and human resources. Identifying responsibilities, grouping them into departments or divisions, and specifying organizational relationships.

Staffing : Staffing deals with providing the right type of persons to man the performance of various functions. Persons are the key to the effective functioning of an organization.

Personnel management has assumed very great importance in modern management studies. Attention is increasingly given to composition of staff, their types and levels, proper recruitment methods and procedures, work distribution and assignment, staff training and development, salary status and career development opportunities, incentives and other related aspects.

Directing : Directing is the managerial function that enables managers to get things done through persons, both individually and collectively. Directing is related to staffing in the sense that these two functions are concerned with employees of the organization. While staffing is concerned with providing and maintaining human resources, directing deals with leading and motivating the human resource to give out the best. It is the most impersonal aspect of management. Directing is not the singular function of the top management. In fact, it pervades throughout the organization at all supervisory levels. This calls for good interpersonal communication both oral and written.

Coordinating : An organization is a total system in which every one of its components must work efficiently and smoothly. The work of an organization is divided into various functional units for efficient performance. It is only through the co-ordinated efforts of all its units, that the organization can achieve its aims and objectives. It is the duty of the managers to coordinate the different functions to avoid any bottleneck.

Reporting: Reporting contains frequently updating the superior authorities and the concerned public about the organization's performance, achievements, shortfalls at regular intervals. The information distribution can be through inspection of official records.

Budgeting : Budgeting is a very important activity encompassing financial planning, accounting and control. Budgets provide information on financial resources and their allocation to different aspects of expenditures. Activities of an organization are assessed in terms of the utilization of the funds provided for that activity. Budgets are usually prepared for a year but estimates of financial resources and expenditure may be prepared for longer period.

SCIENTIFIC MANAGEMENT IN LIBRARIES

In the year 1954, *Library Trends* brought out an Issue with the title 'Scientific Management in Libraries' (Vol. 2(3); Jan 1954). It contained a number of papers on various topics that could be attributed to the application of scientific management in libraries. The editor of the Issue, Ralph R. Shaw, in his 'Introduction' confessed that twenty years ago a similar effort on this subject would not have been possible at all. He was meaning that the subject of scientific management in libraries was not at all ripe then. The papers in this whole Issue of *Library Trends* showed that there was a rapidly growing trend toward the application of scientific management in libraries. During this period, "scientific management had existed primarily as a concept and a mental attitude toward achievement. It consisted of a basic and systematic technique for discovering and establishing objectives, plans, standards, methods, schedules and control of an enterprise, all within the laws of each situation and in an environment of a high morale. It thereby exemplifies the best use of human and material energy". In the references given under all the articles in this issue of *Library Trends,* only 4 items deserve special mention. They were the two items by Donald Coney (1930 and 1952), and one by Paul Howard (1940) and one by Ralph R. Shaw (1947). But paradoxically nowhere there was any reference to Dr. S. R. Ranganathan who had already done the most significant contribution to the subject as early as in 1935.

RANGANATHAN'S CONTRIBUTION TO LIBRARY MANAGEMENT

Dr. Ranganathan's contributions to library management at a time when scientific management was only evolving in the developed countries has to be accepted as the most revolutionary. He brought out his book *Library Administration* in 1935 (second edition in 1955). This book was a remarkable illustration of the application of system analysis, study of work flow, time and motion study, standardization of forms and records, etc. to libraries. In this, he broke down library work into approximately 1,000 or more component jobs. By precisely identifying many different library functions he was able to simplify and streamline all library routines. The book had three parts; Part 1 dealt with the theory of administration, Part 2 dealt with distinctive library functions, and Part 3 was on General Office routines pertaining to libraries. Ranganathan had divided management functions into 8 components, namely,

- Planning,
- Job analysis,
- Routine,
- Elimination of waste,
- Correlation,
- Time Scheme,
- Forms, Registers and Equipment, and
- Correspondence, Files & Records.

Although the book was published half a century ago his ideas serve as practical guidelines even today for operational management in any library. His idea of job analysis was one of the greatest of his contributions in management theory. A routine method is to be set up for doing every job so as to fit them into a time scheme such as hourly, daily, weekly, or monthly routines, and so on. Correlation of different functions and elimination of waste were kept in view in the performance of various routines, designing and use of proper formats for recording information pertaining to various works and jobs, use of appropriate equipment for operational efficiency, ease of handling in the filing of official records, etc. were duly taken care of by Ranganathan. Their relevance today will depend upon their re-orientation in the light of modern management principles and practices, and especially the possibilities of library automation and information technology.

Dr. S.R. Ranganathan had made some original contribution to management discipline, although his main concern was in library management. He divided management function into 8 components, namely Planning, Job analysis, Routine, Elimination of waste, Correlation, Time scheme, Forms, registers and equipment, and Files. (Ranaganathan, (1959).

Modern management is characterized by a scientific approach which involves: (a) the application of scientific methods and analysis to managerial functions and problems; (b) serious consideration of human elements in management, based on psychological studies and behaviour analysis in different situations; (c) increasing emphasis on economic effectiveness in all management functions; (d) a system approach, focusing equal attention on all functions of management; and (e) use of electronic computers for analysis and studies. (IGNOU, 1989).

The discipline of management had many a developments in course of the twentieth century. With the advancement of statistical methods, "quality assurance" and "quality control" became the main stay in management during the 1920s and 1930s. During the 1940s and 1950s, the body of knowledge for doing scientific management evolved into "operations management", "operations research", and "management cybernetics". In the 1980s, "total quality management" became widely popular, growing from quality control techniques. In the 1990s "re-engineering" went from a simple word to a mystique. Many drastic innovations and improvements in scientific management principles and practices were introduced by individual establishments all over the world.

STRATEGIC MANAGEMENT

These days we often hear about Strategic Management (SM) and no discussion about library management can be complete without dealing in that. SM is a relatively new concept in management. This was introduced in the 1970s and 1990; its first phase was Strategic Planning (SP) which was followed by a second phase, namely Strategic Management (SM).

"Strategic Management is a systems approach to identifying and making the necessary changes and measuring the organization's performance as it moves toward its vision. It has been defined as a management system that links strategic planning and decision making with the day-to-day business of operational management" (Gluck, Kaufman and Walleck, 1982).

According to this definition, SP is a precondition for SM. SM, for this purpose, must be understood as *"the process by which the guiding members of an organization envision its future and develop the necessary procedures and operations to achieve that future"* (Goldstein, Nolan and Pfeiffer, 1992). You will come to learn about SP later in Chapter 4 dealing with 'Planning of the Science Information System'. But, here you are going to be told about SM and its application in Library Management.

According to Denise Lindsey Wells, SM can be used to determine the mission, vision, values, goals, objectives, etc. of an organization. The model given below depicts the 5 processes of SM, viz.

- PRE-PLANNING
- STRATEGIC PLANNING
- DEPLOYMENT
- IMPLEMENTATION
- MEASUREMENT & EVALUATION.

SM goes beyond the development of a strategic plan. It is the deployment and implementation of the strategic plan and measurement and evaluation of the results. Measurement & evaluation consist of not only tracking the implementation of actions but, more importantly, assessing how the organization is changing as a result of those actions and using that information to update the plan.

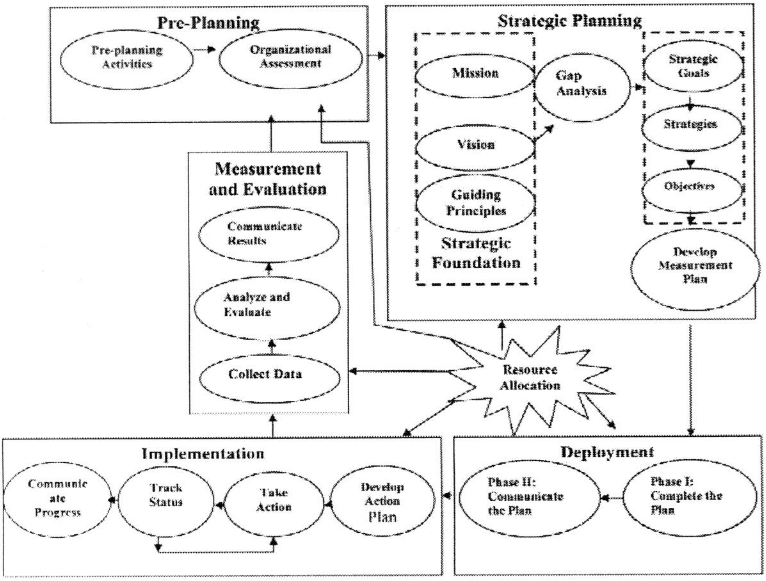

Fig. 1.1. The Strategic Management Model

Source : **Wells, Denise Lindsey,** ***Strategic management for senior leaders: a handbook for implementation*** **(US Dept of Navy TQL Office Publn. No. 96-03).**

STRATEGIC MANAGEMENT IN LIBRARIES

The growing importance of SM in business management discipline has impacted library management also. Recently, there is a growing literature dealing with some aspect or the other of SM in libraries. According to Joseph R. Mathews (2005), "*Strategic Management consists of the analysis, decisions, and actions an organization undertakes in order to create and sustain competitive advantage*". You can find two elements in this definition:

One is that SM entails three ongoing processes: *analysis*, *decisions*, and *actions*. Analysis is of the goals (vision, mission, and strategic objectives) along with the analysis of the internal and external environment of the organization (as in the case with SWOT analysis). Decisions are the strategic decisions that the leaders must take. Decisions address two questions: What to compete in? And how to compete in? - These questions also involve an organization's domestic and international operations. Then come the actions. Decisions are of no use unless they are acted upon.

The second element in the definition of Mathews is that the essence of SM is the study of why do some firms outperform others? Managers need to determine how their firm is to compete advantageously and sustainably? This involves two fundamental questions: How to create competitive advantage in the market place? – whether by cost reduction or by developing unique products? Sustainable competitive advantage cannot be achieved through operational effectiveness alone, because everyone may be doing the same. Strategy is about being different from everyone else; performing similar activities in different ways. A company with a good strategy must make clear choices about what it wants to accomplish. Trying to do everything that your rivals do eventually leads to mutually destructive price competition, and not long term advantage. For example, companies like Wall–Mart, South West Airlines, and IKEA are reported to have developed unique, internally consistent, and difficult to imitate systems that have provided with sustainable competitive advantage.

The ultimate objective of SM should be to attain competitive advantage for your library or your services. Unlike as in the past, libraries and information systems today have to operate in a competitive environment where the end users have many new options particularly because of the expanding digital universe where access to information and documents is literally at finger tips and round the clock. As pointed out earlier, there is no point in doing the self same thing as many other libraries do. Competitive advantage can be achieved only through uniqueness in either product or service. The strategic part of library management is in making clear choices about what your library wants to accomplish. This involves all the 3 steps listed earlier, viz. analysis, decisions and actions (Mathews, 2005).

REFERENCES

CONEY, Donald. (1930), 'Scientific management and university libraries' in Schwenning, G.T. *Management problems*, University of North Carolina, 1930, pp.168-198.

CONEY, Donald. (1952), 'Management in college and university libraries' *Library Trends*, vol.1 July 1952 pp.83-94.

DRUCKER, PETER (1973), *Management: tasks, responsibilities, practices*, Heinemann, 1973

FAYOL, Henri (1916), *General and industrial administration*, (French original), Paris, H. Dumond, 1916, (and English translation in 1949).

GOODSTEIN, L.D., NOLAN, T.M. & PFEIFFER, J.W. (1992), *Applied strategic planning; a comprehensive guide*, San Diego, CA Pfeiffer & Co, 1992.

GULICK, L.H. (1937) : "Notes on the Theory of Organization" in L. Gulick & L. Urwick (eds), *Papers on the Science of Administration*, New York, Institute of Public Administration, Pp3-45.

GLUCK, F.W., KAUFMAN, S & WALLECK, A.S. (1982), 'The four phases of strategic management', *Journal of Business Strategy*, 2(3), 1982 pp.9-21.

HOWARD, Paul (1940), 'The functions of library management, *Library Quarterly* vol.10, July 1940 pp.313-349.

IGNOU (1989), *Library Management, Course BLS-2*, New Delhi, Indira Gandhi National Open University, P.6.

MASON, Merilyn Gell (1999), *Strategic management for today's libraries*, ALA, 1999.

MATHEWS, Joseph R. (2005), *Strategic planning and management for library managers*, Greenwood, USA, 2005.

RANGANATHAN, S.R. (1959): *Library Administration*, Edn.2, Bombay, Asia Publishing House.

SHAW, Ralph R. (1947), 'Scientific management in the library' *Wilson Library*

Bulletin, Vol 21, January 1947 pp.349-352.

SHAW, Ralph R. (1954), 'Introduction' *Library Trends*, Vol. 2 (3); January 1954.pp

SHERA, Jessy H. (1972) Foundations for Education for Librarianship, Becker & Hayes.

TAYLOR, Frederick Winslow (1909/1911), The *Principles of Scientific Management*, , Harper & Brothers Publishers 1919.

WELLS, Denise Lindsey (1998), Strategic management for senior leaders: a handbook for implementation, U.S. Dept of Navy Total Quality Leadership Office Publication No. 92-03.

2

Science Information Systems

'Science Information Systems' is a composite concept, where the three constituent terms viz. 'science', 'information' and 'systems' are combined to give a special meaning and scope. To understand this concept better one should know: what is science? what is information? what is science information? what is a system? what is an information system, and finally, what is the science information system?

WHAT IS SCIENCE?

The term 'science' is very familiar and it is used to distinguish certain subject areas / disciplines from others. But, what is the distinguishing feature of a science discipline? In other words a question may be posed: 'what makes science a science?'

Science is an area of human activity wherein a procedure called the Scientific Method is employed for invention and discovery of a new knowledge, or the expansion or modification of an already existing knowledge. So, what makes science a science is whether the subject field has the potential, or not, for the application of the scientific method in its development. If that is so, what exactly is the so called 'scientific method'?

SCIENTIFIC METHOD

It is the special method of sciences which comprises in a set of procedures whereby a given phenomenon is subjected to systematic studies and the ultimate truth of the matter is sought to be established. It is a method of procedure that has characterized natural science since the 17th century, consisting in systematic observation, measurement, and experiment, and the formulation, testing and modification of hypotheses. The whole process of Scientific Method may be described as follows:

- Observation of the phenomenon
- Drawing generalizations
- Testing the generalization based on further observations
- Formulation of a Hypothesis
- Testing of the Hypothesis through further observations or experimentation
- Formulation of a Theory
- Testing of the theory based on further observations or experimentation.
- Formulation of Laws

The process of the scientific method involves making conjectures (hypotheses), deriving predictions from them as logical consequences, and then carrying out experiments of empirical observations based on those predictions. A hypothesis is a conjecture, based on knowledge obtained while seeking answers to the question.

A linearized, pragmatic scheme of the main steps involved in scientific method is sometimes offered as a guideline for research procedure:

1. Observe the phenomena, understand the problem and define a question;
2. Do background research and Gather information and resources on work already done (further observation);

3. Form an explanatory hypothesis;
4. Analyze the data;
5. Interpret the data and draw conclusions and refine the hypothesis that serve as a starting point for new hypothesis;
6. Publish results; and
7. Retest (frequently done by other scientists).

Science is, therefore, systematized human knowledge and it consists of various disciplines, some of which are traditionally accepted like Mathematics, Physics, Chemistry, Botany, and Zoology. Some others are applications of these basic disciplines as are Engineering, Medicine, Agriculture, and Animal Husbandry. Further, there are some modern disciplines that have taken shape from the mutual relationship of different old or new disciplines. Such inter-disciplinary developments and formation of new subjects are conspicuous characters of present day science. The modes of formation of new disciplines are an area of specialized investigation for library and information science students, at least in India.

Strictly speaking, the term science denotes all subjects and disciplines where the Scientific Method is employed. The scientist observes the phenomena, formulates some hypothesis, tests the hypotheses based on further observation and experimentation and finally arrive at the indispensable truth. If science is the study of phenomena to discover their truth, depending upon the nature of the phenomena studied science can have different divisions. Science can study physical, natural and social phenomena. Disciplines dealing with studies of physical and natural phenomena are generally referred to by the term 'Science'. These are also the science disciplines that are earlier in origin, or mostly referred to as 'sciences' traditionally. But, when phenomena studied are social or human, the disciplines formed from them are known as "Social Science". Just as there are divisions like Natural

Sciences, Physical Sciences and Social Sciences there are also divisions like Pure Sciences or Basic Sciences, and Applied Sciences.

THE SPIRAL OF SCIENTIFIC METHOD

Dr. S. R. Ranganathan has given the Spiral of Scientific Method which is a visual picture of the four phases of research, namely, Empirical (data collection) Hypothesizing (Inductive logic), Deductive (Deduction of laws) and Verification (Testing of results). To quote at length from Dr Ranganathan's own words:

> "Scientific Method is characterized by a never-ending spiral movement, It is schematically represented in the diagram ... The cycle implied in the spiral will be followed in the clock-wise direction. For convenience of reference, the four cardinal points of the cycle are denoted by the

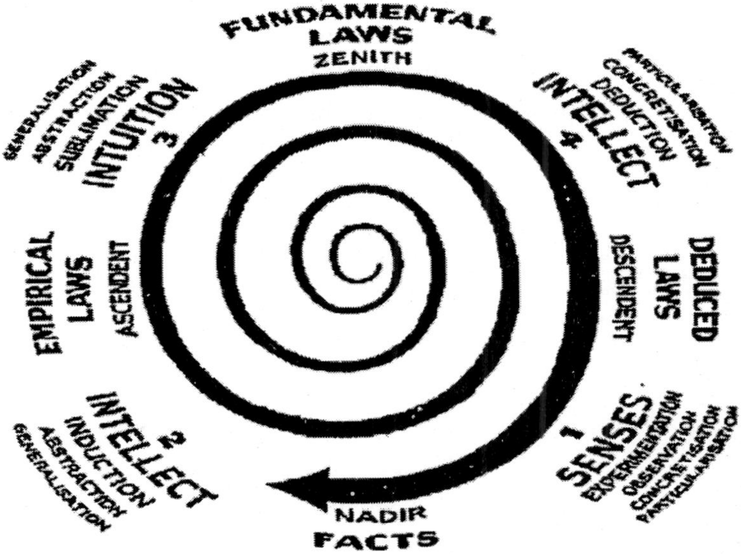

Fig. 2.1 . Dr Ranganathan's Spiral of Scientific Method

terms Nadir, Ascendent, Zenith, and Descendent. The nadir marks the accumulation of facts, obtained by observation, experimentation, and other forms of experience. The ascendent marks the accumulation of inducted or empirical laws got out of the facts accumulated at the nadir, by inductive logic including normal equations and other aids from statistical calculus. The zenith marks the fundamental laws formulated with the aid of intuition of some degree or other, so as to comprehend all the inducted or empirical laws accumulated at the ascendent as compelling implications. The descendent marks the accumulation of the deduced laws got from the fundamental laws at the zenith, with the aid of deductive logic including general semantics and all kinds of mathematical calculuses.

The four cardinal points give rise to four quadrants in the cycle implied in the spiral. For convenience of reference, the quadrants will be numbered 1 to 4 respectively, as follows: Quadrant 1 is the one between descendant and nadir; Quadrant 2 is the one between nadir and ascendent; Quadrant 3 is the one between ascendent and zenith, and Quadrant 4 is the one between zenith and descendent." (Ranganathan,1988).

Dr. Ranganathan has quoted Karl Pearson (1911) to define the scope of science as follows: "*The field of science is unlimited; its material is endless, every group of natural phenomena, every phase of social life, every stage of past or present development is material for science*".

The three definitions of the term "science" that follow reflect the generalized view of its subject of study:

1. "A system based or purporting to be based upon scientific principles; a method of arrangement,

functioning, etc, reconciling practical or utilitarian ends with scientific laws: e.g. Domestic Science, Animal Husbandry".

2. "Accumulated and accepted knowledge which has been systematised and formulated with reference to the general truths and made available in work, life, or the search of truth",

3. "A branch of study which is concerned either with a connected body of demonstrated truths or with observed facts systematically classified and more or less collected by being brought under general laws and which includes trustworthy methods for the discovery of new truth within its own domain" (Ranganathan, 1988).

Science is therefore, systematized human knowledge and it consists of various disciplines, some of which are traditionally accepted like Mathematics, Physics, Chemistry, Botany, and Zoology. Some others are applications of these basic disciplines as are Engineering, Medicine, Agriculture, and Animal Husbandry. Further, there are some modern disciplines that have taken shape out of the mutual relationship of different old or new disciplines. Such inter-disciplinary developments and formation of new subjects are conspicuous characters of present day science. The modes of formation of new disciplines are an area of specialized investigation for library and information science students, at least in India.

Strictly speaking, the term science denotes all subjects and disciplines where the Scientific Method is employed. The scientist observes the phenomena, formulates some hypothesis, tests the hypotheses based on further observation and experimentation and finally arrive at the indispensable truth. If science is the study of phenomena to discover their truth, depending upon the nature of the phenomena studied science can have different divisions. Science can study physical, natural and social phenomena. Disciplines dealing with studies of physical and natural phenomena are generally referred to by the term 'Science'. These are also the science disciplines that are earlier in origin, or mostly referred to as 'sciences' traditionally. But, when phenomena studied are social or human, the disciplines formed from them are known as "Social Science". Just as there are divisions like Natural Sciences, Physical Sciences and Social Sciences there are also divisions like Pure Sciences or Basic Sciences, and Applied Sciences.

SCIENCE AND TECHNOLOGY

'Science' is spoken of very often in combination with 'technology', as 'science and technology'. Mostly, the term 'technology' is used to mean the development and application of knowledge gained from the science studies, in the production and use of goods and associated services. Therefore, in common parlance, 'technology' is understood as application of science. Also therefore, the expression 'science and technology, means the entire spectrum of science including its basic, applied and developmental levels of knowledge.

WHAT IS INFORMATION?

'Information' is defined by dictionaries, as knowledge, intelligence, facts or data which can be used, transferred or communicated, from one to another. This being the more common sense meaning of the term, this is also the sense in which librarians and others engaged in the field of information storage and retrieval often use the term 'information'. Jesse H. Shera's famous definition of information is, "*it is that which is transmitted by the act or process of communication, it may be a message, a signal or a stimulus*" (Shera, 1972). We know that man communicates in many ways – either in non-verbal or verbal modes. While there can be many models of non-verbal communication none of them involve the use of a language or words. Verbal communication, on the other hand, involves necessarily the use of a language or a system of words. In that sense, verbal communication can be either oral or written. Verbal communication is through more or less permanent packets of intelligible information in such forms as: writing, printing, drawing, sound recordings, instrument traces (as in the case of an ECG record), electronic records like all computer readable tapes, cassettes, hard disks, diskettes, CDs, DVDs, etc., and in the later stage the many digitized items that could be either used offline or online. All of these varied items can be called by a generic name "Recorded Information". Librarians and information specialists have to be mainly concerned with these packets of recorded information.

IMPORTANCE OF INFORMATION

Information of the kind mentioned above has great importance in the society. It has many and varied uses – for example in education, research and development, in business, industry and trade, in government and public administration, in the economic, political and social life of the individual, in defense, war, diplomacy and peace, in international understanding, in development and culture, etc. There is hardly any area in the life and development of an individual or society where information input in some form or other is not involved. Information is an important ingredient in the decision making process, and human beings are always, voluntarily or involuntarily, making decisions in big or small situations which affect their own lives or of others in the society. Incorrect, or inadequate information input will lead only to wrong decisions, and the consequence of wrong decisions may become detrimental to the individual and the society in different degrees.

If information is that much important and useful, the required information must be made available to all, in the manner and style they need them. The society must find ways and means of collecting, storing, organizing and distributing information to the people according to their varied requirements. Such efforts at collecting, storing and maintaining recorded information, for the present or future use, started in the society as early as human beings began to write and keep records. At first they took the shape of the archives, later the manuscript libraries, still later the libraries of printed books – the various institutions founded by society to keep and care for records. With the advent and growth of the modern libraries and professional librarianship, several sophisticated institutions and services have sprung up for catering to the specialized information needs of the people. Thus came to be established:

- Special Libraries,
- Documentation Centres,
- Information Centres,
- Information Analysis Centres,
- Referral Centres,
- Information Storage and Retrieval Systems,
- Data bases or Data banks, etc. .

The purpose of all these establishments was to collect information needed for specific purposes and to promote their effective use. All these can be generally called '**information systems**'

WHAT IS AN INFORMATION SYSTEM?

An 'information system', therefore, can be defined as some deliberate arrangement made for the storage and retrieval of information by collecting, organizing, and making accessible the records of all relevant information to those who need them. An information system is an organized combination of people, hardware, software, communications, networks, and data resources that collects, transforms, and disseminates information in an organization. It is a set of interrelated components that collect, manipulate, store data and disseminate information and provide a feedback mechanism to monitor performance. It is a combination of hardware, software, infrastructure and trained personnel organized to facilitate planning, control, coordination, and decision making in an organization. The components that must be combined together in order to produce an information system are: People, Hardware, Software, Data, Network, Procedures, and Feedback.

The purpose of all these systems is to collect all information needed for specific purposes and to promote their use. All kinds of organizations, industrial companies, government establishments, business firms or R&D institutions have been giving increasing attention to the design and development of information systems to meet their complex information needs. It may also help the manager and workers to analyze problems, visualize complex subjects and create new products.

In later years, these individual efforts at building up and maintaining information systems have led to the creation of integrated information systems and networks, first as Local Area Networks, then as Wide Area Networks, and later as regional / national / international networks, finally leading to the establishment of the World Wide Web and Internet.

IMPORTANCE OF SCIENTIFIC INFORMATION

Information, speaking generally. is an essential resource both for the society and the individual, comparable to the resources of nature, like land, minerals and water; like resources of capital, labour, intellectual manpower and human skills. Whoever has the proper information is in an advantageous position over others who do not have that information. If this is true, scientific information is a more vital resource because today science and society are so intertwined, so to say that the present society of ours is a scientific and technological society.

Scientific information is the result of scientific research at different levels: (a) basic and fundamental research; and (b) applied or practical research. Results of research at both levels are significant information for the society. The results of basic research are of direct interest mainly to other research workers, either at the basic research level or at the applied research level. But they are not of any direct application or significance to the common man, other than for satisfying the curiosity of general knowledge. The results of applied research and development concern virtually all types of information users. Since scientific research is a cumulative and inter-dependent activity information is significant as Input and Output in every research. Therefore, Science Information Systems are a crucial part of the science and technology set up in any country or for the world as a whole.

PURPOSE OF A SCIENCE INFORMATION SYSTEM

Some of the frequently stated purposes of a science information system are the following:

- To collect, conserve, and organize information sources and materials;
- To expedite the utilization of information;
- To eliminate unnecessary duplication or gaps in research;
- To provide access to the informational materials in one's fields;
- To improve the coverage and the timeliness of information transfer process;
- To maximize the use of available subject specialists and increase their efficiency;
- To overcome the language barrier in scientific communication;
- To ensure participation in joint ventures;

- To establish comprehensive inventory of world literature in the respective fields.

REFERENCES

PEARSON, Karl, (1911), *Grammar of Science. (originally published in 1892) Edn.3, Adam & Charles black, 1911*

RANGANATHAN, S.R. (1959): *Library Administration,* Edn.2, Bombay, Asia Publishing House.

RANGANATHAN, S.R. (1988), *The Five Laws of Library Science*, Bangalore, Sarada Ranganathan Endowment For Library Science.

SHERA, Jessy H. (1972) *Foundations for Education for Librarianship*, Becker & Hayes.

3
Science and Technology Set Up in India

SCIENTIFIC HERITAGE OF INDIA

India has a long and distinguished tradition in science and technology from the very ancient times, beginning from the period of Indus Valley Civilization which dates back to 3000 BC or so. Being the youngest and the largest of the four ancient civilizations, (namely the Mesopotamian, the Egyptian, the Greeco-Roman, and the Indus Valley civilizations), it was a full-fledged civilization, firmly settled in the areas of modern Baluchistan, Sind and Punjab that were lying in the broad plains and valleys of the lower Indus River. This region was, in those days, a far more fertile one than today, with much heavier rainfalls and dense forests. The excavations conducted in the sites of the two metropolitan cities and other towns in the Indus Valley, like Mohenjo-daro, Harappa (both are now in Pakistan), Kalibangan (in Rajasthan), and Lothel (in Gujarat) have brought to light salient data and information about India's great scientific heritage. Lothel, for example, was a port town which showed evidences of comparably advanced knowledge and technology in matters like town planning, metallurgy, arts and crafts. For example, their dwelling places were built with standard size burnt out bricks, tiled floorings, and interlinked drainage system. Uses made of ceramics, terracotta craft, bangles and beads making, solid wheel carts, and copper-bronze craftsmanship, etc. were detected. The circle and the wheel had already become part of the life of the people. Lothel is reported to have a dockyard with the largest maritime structure ever built by a Bronze Age community, with its warehouses, commercial streets, ship building industry, etc. All these show the wide ranging technical skills required for an enriched community living. The technicians might have enjoyed a significant status in that society. The scientific ideas, especially in Geometry, was evidenced by the town planning and standardization techniques followed, which were of a high order.

The Post-Aryan Period

The Aryan invasion during the second millennium BC devastated all the marks of the great Indus Valley civilization. What followed was a dark age in the history of India. About this dark period *Rig-Veda* was the unique source of information. The Aryan invasion caused a slow transition from the old tribal to a new feudal society and the Aryan India emerged out of the Dark Ages probably after the middle of the second millennium BC. *Vedas* was the first literary work of the Indian Aryans. The Vedic literature contained also the scientific and technical knowledge of the people of India. The philosophical wisdom and scientific inventions of Indians were generally noticed and reported by foreign scholars. Notable contributions were identified in the fields of Astronomy, Mathematics, Medicine, Metal working, and other techniques. These achievements of the Indians attracted the attention of knowledge-seekers especially from the West Asia and medieval Europe.

Indian Mathematics

The most fundamental contribution of ancient Indians to Mathematics was undoubtedly the "decimal system of

promoted conservation and communication of knowledge and ideas.

SCIENCE IN MODERN INDIA

In the history of modern India, the period prior to her independence was crucially important as she was mainly under the British rule when the foundation for a future higher education and scientific and technological research was almost laid. Prior to independence, research in India was largely in Pure Sciences. This began with the establishment of the Royal Asiatic Society of Bengal in 1784, which was followed by the Trigonometric Survey of India (1818), the Geological Survey of India (1831), the Meteorological Department of India (1875), the Botanical Survey of India (1890), and the C.S.I.R. (1942). Nevertheless, at the time of independence the S&T infrastructure of India was neither strong nor organized as of the developed countries. Because of this reason, India was technologically dependent on other countries. But, after independence, India had, in her avowed pursuit of self-reliance, tremendous growth in the sphere of science & technology education and research. From 1950 onwards through the successive Five Year Plans the Government of India could establish a number of Research & Development Laboratories in various sectors of science and technology, like Health, Agriculture, Atomic Energy, Space Science, etc. Examples are: the Bhabha Atomic Research Centre (1957), the Indian National Committee for Space Research (INCOSPAR, 1962), etc.

PRESENT S & T INFRASTRUCTURE OF INDIA

To quote from *India 2011*, "*Scientific and technological activities in India are carried out under a wide set-up consisting of Central Government, State Governments, higher educational sector, public and private sector industry and non-profit institutions / associations. These institutional structures with their research laboratories, are the main contributors to research and development being carried out in the country. Notable among these are: the Council of Scientific and Industrial Research (CSIR), Indian Council of Agricultural Research (ICAR), and Indian Council of Medical Research (ICMR). In addition, there are many laboratories of various departments / ministries, viz. Department of Atomic Energy, Ministry of Information Technology, Department of Space, Ministry of Earth Sciences, Defense Research and Development Organization, Ministry of Environment and Forests, Ministry of New and Renewable Energy Sources, and the Ministry of Science and Technology. Further, there are over 1200 in-house research and development units in industrial undertakings supporting research in their respective industries. Many Indian universities and deemed universities, such as IITs, also undertake substantial research and development work"* (p.833). The following chart will indicate the various Ministries and Departments in the Government of India that are directly involved in Science & Technology activities:

- **Ministry of Science & Technology**
  - * Dept. of Science & Technology (DSTR)
  - * Dept. of Scientific & Industrial Research (DSIR),
    - — CSIR and National Laboratories
  - * Dept. of Atomic Energy
  - * Dept. of Space
  - * Dept. of Biotechnology
- **Ministry of Earth Sciences**
  - * Dept. of Ocean Development (DOD)
- **Ministry of Defence (DRDO)**
- **Ministry of Health & Family Welfare**
  - * Indian Council of Medical Research (ICMR)
- **Ministry of Education**
  - * University Grants Commission (UGC)
    - — Universities & Colleges
- **Ministry of Agriculture**
  - * Indian Council of Agricultural Research (ICAR)

— Agricultural Universities

- **Ministry of Environment, Forest & Climate Change (MoEFCC)**
  - * Botanical Survey of India (BSI)
  - * Zoological Survey of India (ZSI)
  - * Forest Survey of India (FSI)
  - * Environmental Research
- **Ministry of Communications**
  - * Dept. of Posts (DOP)
  - * Dept. of Telecommunication (DOT)
- **Ministry of Electronics and Information Technology**
  - * Dept. of Information Technology (DIT)

Fig. 3.1. Chart showing Science & Technology Set Up in Government of India

MIINISTRY OF SCIENCE & TECHNOLOGY

The Ministry of Science & Technology has a number of departments, namely Department of Science & Technology, Department of Scientific and Industrial Research, Department of Atomic Energy, Department of Space, and Department of Bio-technology. Each of them has its own S&T programmes. The following sections will give you some salient features of these entities of the Ministry of Science and Technology.

Department of Science and Technology (DST)

The DST was set up in 1971 with the objective of promoting research in new areas and to play the role of a nodal department for organizing, coordinating and promoting science and technology activities in the country. Over the years, DST has evolved policy statements and guidelines, provided mechanisms for co-ordination in the areas of science and technology in which a number of institutions have interests and capabilities, and supported scientific institutions and professional bodies through grant-in-aids. DST has played a catalytic and coordinating role and in this process over the past few years, the efforts at promoting science and technology in the States and Union Territories have also gathered considerable momentum.

During the VI Five Year Plan period initiative was taken for the development of State Councils for Science and Technology, the constitution of the Technology Development Board in 1996 with a view to provide financial assistance to industrial concerns and other agencies for developing and applying indigenous technology, the Science Communication and Popularization through the establishment of National Council for Science and Technology Commission, and about 18 autonomous scientific institutions supported by the DST, including the Sree Chithra Thirunal Institute for Medical Sciences and Technology, Trivandrum. DST also extends financial and administrative support to several academies and professional bodies which are engaged in the promotion of S&T in the country like the Indian Academy of Sciences, Bangalore, through the involvement of scientists and engineers.

With the objective of developing indigenous technology and utilizing imported technology as appropriate national priorities GoI had formulated the Technology Policy Statement in 1983.. This led to the development of an industrial policy for India. Then, in order to build a blue print for future programmes of S &T, and to give a direction to the initiative to be undertaken, the GOI announced the Science and Technology Policy, 2003. The policy outlines the approach to S&T governance, optimal utilization of existing physical knowledge resources, development of innovative technologies, systems and technologies for migration and management of natural hazards, generation and management of intellectual property and creation of awareness amongst general masses about the uses and benefits of science & technology. The various programmes and activities of the DST are listed below:

- R& D Programmes
- Infrastructure Development
- Human Resources Development
- Technology Development and Related Programmes
- Technology Development Board
- S & T Programmes for Socio-Economic Development
- National Resources Data Management Systems
- National Spatial Data Infrastructure (NSDI)
- State S & T Programmes
- Science Communication and Popularization
- S & T Resources Information
- International Cooperation
- Survey of India
- National Atlas and Thematic Mapping Organization
- Autonomous Scientific Institutions

(For more details see *India 2011; a Reference Annual* or its later editions):

Science, Technology and Innovation Policy, 2013

In 2013 the GoI brought out its Science, Technology and Innovation Policy. To quote from *India 2020*: "*The new Science, Technology and Innovation (STI) Policy unveiled in 2013 includes a thrust for innovations in science and technology sector. STI policy reveals an aspiration to gain global competitiveness and link science sector to the developmental agenda of the country. Science, research and innovation system for high technology led path for India (SRISHTI) is the main policy goal. Integration of science, research and innovation systems and emergence of India as one of the top five of six knowledge powers in science are expressed aspirations of the new STI policy. To translate this vision into action, the Department has already established a dedicated Policy Research Cell. Five policy research centres in academic institutions have been established to develop and design new programmes and action plans for implementation in science, technology and innovation sector in the country"* (*India 2020*, P.497).

Department of Scientific & Industrial Research (DSIR)

The primary endeavour of DSIR is to promote R&D by the industries, support a larger cross section of small and medium industrial units to develop state-of-the-art globally competitive technologies of high commercial potential, catalyze faster commercialization of lab-scale R&D, enhance the share of technology intensive exports in overall exports, strengthen industrial consultancy and technology management capabilities and establish user friendly information network to facilitate scientific and industrial research in the country.

It also provides a link between scientific laboratories and industrial establishments for transfer of technologies through National Research Development Corporation (NRDC) and facilitates investment in R&D through Central Electronics Limited (CEL) (*www.anusandhan.net*). DSIR has the mandate for indigenous technology promotion, development and utilization. It primarily encourages industry to increase their share in the country's R&D expenditures, to nurture the innovative spirit of individuals by helping them to convert their ideas into models/ prototypes and then to products, and to demonstrate the state-of-the-art globally competitive technologies. DSIR implements the plan scheme "Technology Promotion, Development and Utilization (TPDU) Programme", and co-ordinates the activities of two autonomous bodies, namely the Council of Scientific and Industrial Research (CSIR) and the Consultancy Development Centre (CDC) and two public sector undertakings, the National Research Development Corporation (NRDC) and the Central Electronics Limited (CEL).

CSIR & National Laboratories

The CSIR is an autonomous R & D organization founded in 1942 under the DSIR with the objective of providing scientific and industrial R&D to maximize the economic, environmental and societal benefits to the people of India. It is a multi-disciplinary, multi-location set-up comprising of 38 National Laboratories, 39 Outreach Centres, 3 Innovation Complexes and 5 Units throughout the nation Its R & D expertise and experience is embodied in about 4,600 active scientists supported by about 8,000 scientific and technical personnel (*CSIR Annual Report 2014*).

CSIR aims at achieving excellence in science; global competitiveness in technology based on high science; and innovation in all spheres of activities from science to technology. CSIR has been an active provider of technologies for industrial competitiveness, S&T base for strategic sector; technology for societal welfare and science for advancement of knowledge. Some of the areas of active involvement and commitment of CSIR have been: Aerospace Science and Technology, Biology and Biotechnology, Chemical technology, Earth Science and technology, Ecology and environment, Electronics, Food, Health, Housing, Information, Materials and engineering, New Millennium Indian Technology Leadership, Human Resource Development, etc. CSIR has recently regrouped and repositioned its key sectors of knowledge and technology generation into five clusters which are: Biological Sciences, Chemical Sciences; Engineering Sciences; Physical Sciences, Information Sciences and CSIR 800. By the last mentioned cluster, CSIR recognizes that S&T inputs significantly contribute to improve the quality of life of the Indian masses comprising 800 million, through small scale enterprises. CSIR under its New Millennium Indian Technology Initiative (NMITI) is operating two categories of projects: (a) Nationally evolved projects (NEP), and Industry originated projects

(IOP), with a view to yield new cutting edge technologies that are globally competitive, or to establish globally new technology paradigms for industry that are sustainable and eco-friendly. CSIR is contributing significantly to the development of highly qualified personnel in diverse disciplines of S&T in the country. For this, it identifies budding talents, who have aptitude and aspirations to work for the generation of new knowledge, provide them with opportunities in the field of scientific and industrial research, and encourage them by granting Fellowships and Awards. CSIR is also spearheading the Intellectual Property Management movement in the country.

During 2009-10 it has filed 175 patents abroad and 159 patents in India. It has a portfolio of 2,349 patents in India and 3,054 patents abroad. CSIR has published 4,234 research papers in SCI journals with an average 2.28 impact factor per paper. CSIR has filed 2413 patent applications during the period between 2009 and 2019 out of which 1917 were granted. It has created and is the custodian of Traditional Knowledge Digital Library (TKDL) as a weapon against unethical commercial exploitation of Indian traditional knowledge.

Department of Atomic Energy (DAE)

The DAE was established in 1954 and is now an integrated group of organizations and comprises five research centres, three Industrial Organizations, five Public Sector Undertakings, and three Service Organizations. It also supports seven institutes of international repute, engaged in research in basic science, astronomy, astrophysics, cancer research, education, etc. and a society that provides educational facilities to the children of DAE employees. DAE has ambitious nuclear programmes that aim at achieving an installed nuclear power capacity of 22,480 MWE by the year 2031 on completion of projects (as per information supplied to Lok Sabha on 4th March 2020 by the Union Minister of State Sri

Jitendra Singh). Within the next 5 years a capacity of 5,300 MW is proposed to be added on progressive completion of nuclear power plants at Kakrapar in Gujarat, Rawatbhata in Rajasthan and Kudankulam in Tamil Nadu. The Nuclear Power Corporation of India (NPCIL), a public sector undertaking of DAE, is responsible for the design, construction and operation of nuclear power reactors. It now operates 18 reactors with an installed capacity of 4,340 MWe. With its new projects the installed capacity was expected to reach 6,780 MWe in 2008. The DAE organizations contributing to the Nuclear Fuel Cycle Programme are the Atomic Minerals Directorate for Research and Exploration (AMD), Hyderabad, the Uranium Corporation of India Ltd (UCIL), the Jaduguda, Nuclear Fuel Complex (FC), Hyderabad, the Heavy Water Board (HWB), Mumbai, the Bhabha Atomic Research Centre (BARC), Trombay and the Indira Gandhi Centre for Atomic Research (IGCAR), Mumbai. The Nuclear Power Programme of DAE is envisaged in three successive stages, namely, Pressurized Heavy Water Reactors, Fast Breeder Plutonium based reactors, and Thorium based reactors. DAE's programme relating to radiation technologies and application covers building and operation of research reactors for production of radioisotopes, and other sources of radiation such as accelerators and lasers, and developing and deploying radiation technology applications in the field of medicine, agriculture and industry. The Nuclear Agriculture Programme of DAE focuses on the use of radiation technology for the development of high yielding crop seed, radiation processing of food items, fertilizer and pesticide-related studies and other areas. In the sphere of Nuclear Medicine and Health Care the radioisotopes and their formulation find wide applications in diagnosis, therapy and health care. BARC and BRITS (the Board of Radiation & Isotope Technology, Kalpakkam) are the main centres of this activity. Laser systems and Electron Beam Accelerators are the two areas where India is one of the front runners. The Raja

Ramanna Centre for Advanced Technology (RRCAT) in Indore, and BARC in Trombay are engaged in the development of Laser systems, Electron Beam processes and devices, and Plasma devices. DAE research centres are also engaged in basic research in areas relevant to their programmes. Some of the autonomous research institutes supported by grant-in-aid by DAE are centres of excellence in basic research. They are spread over disciplines like Mathematics & Computation, Physics, Seismic Studies, Superconductivity, Astronomy, Chemistry, and Biology, For example are institutions like: the Harish Chandra Research Institute, Allahabad, Institute of Mathematical Sciences at Chennai, the Institute of Physics, Bhubaneshwar, the National Centre for Biological Sciences, Bangalore, the Saha Institute of Nuclear Physics, the Homi Bhabha National Institute, Mumbai having the status of a 'deemed University', etc. that are some of the institutions of repute coming under umbrella of the DAE.

Department of Space

Today, India is one of the few countries which have an impressive array of achievements in the area of space research. Space activities in India were initiated with the setting up of the Indian National Commission for Space Research (INCOSPAR) in 1962. In the same year work on Thumba Equatorial Rocket Launching Station (TERLS) in Trivandrum was also started. The Indian Space Research Organization (ISRO) was established in 1969. Later in 1972, the Space Commission and the Department of Space (DOS) came into existence and the ISRO was placed under DOS. During the 1970s, only experimental satellite programmes like Aryabhatta, Bhaskara, Rohini and Apple could be launched, but during the 1980s operational satellites like INSAT (Indian National Satellite system) and IRS (Indian Remote Sensing Satellite) could be launched and put into use. These two are the major programmes of ISRO. The INSAT system, established in 1983, is a joint venture of the Department of Space, Department of

Telecommunication, the Indian Meteorological Department, All India Radio and Doordarshan. Today, satellites built by ISRO have become an integral part of our national infrastructure. The major operational space systems of ISRO today are the INSAT, the IRS, the PSLV (Polar Satellite Launch Vehicles), and the GSLV (Geosynchronous Satellite Launch Vehicles). INSAT is the largest domestic communication satellite system in the Asia Pacific Region with 11 satellites in operation. Today, a total of 650 Earth stations and nearly 119,000 VSATs telecommunication terminals are supported by the INSAT system. INSAT also has facilitated expansion of television coverage in India so as to have satellite television coverage of 100% area and 100% population. Through ISRO's Telemedicine Network super specialty medical services have become available to the remote and rural population by enabling 382 hospitals, 306 Remote district/ health centres. The launch of EDUSAT, the satellite of India dedicated exclusively for educational services through the INSAT system has networked about 60,000 class rooms in the various academic institutions and universities. INSAT system is also providing meteorological services through Very High Resolution Radiometer and cameras attached to some of its spacecrafts. Indian Remote Sensing Satellite system is one of the largest constellations of remote sensing satellites in operation in the world today. ISRO's PSLV and GSLV programmes, have enabled India to make tremendous strides in launch technology to achieve self-reliance in that specialty. Thus, the developments in space research have been spectacular, particularly in its Launch Vehicles Programme, until the successful launching of an advanced communication satellite into the orbit for the first time, in April 2010, by using the own cryogenic engine developed by Indian scientists. Similarly, the Chandrayan-1 being India's first mission to moon, was successfully launched in October 2008 with the path-breaking discovery of the traces of water in the lunar surface. The

Chandrayan-2 Mission and its successful accomplishment in 2019 was a remarkable achievement of Indian space programme as it marked a significant technological leap compared to the previous missions of ISRO.

India has now a vibrant space science programme covering Astronomy, Astrophysics, Planetary Science and Exploration, and Solar Terrestrial Physics including Space Weather, Space Meteorology and Climate and Microgravity science/applications. As part of that programme, all ground facilities have been built up. Today, the ISRO activities are spread over the different parts of India and located in 18 places at least, namely, Thiruvananthapuram, Mahendragiri, Bangalore, Hassan, Sriharikotta, Thirupati, Hyderabad, Mumbai, Nagpur, Kharaghpur, Bhopal, Ahmedabad, Shillong, Jodhpur, Lucknow, New Delhi, Dehra Dun, and Chandigarh. There are about 27 ISRO Centres under individual names including the Indian Institute of Space Science & Technology (IIST), a deemed university, which was established at Thiruvananthapuram in 2007.

Indian Space programme on the whole has many activities and applications. Six launch vehicle missions were successfully accomplished. ISRO could place five Indian satellites into the orbit. These included one earth observation satellite, three communication satellites, and one navigation satellite. In all ISRO accomplished 13 missions which includes six launch vehicle missions, six satellite missions and one technology demonstrator, Pad Abort test.One of the unique characteristics of Indian space programme has been the application-oriented efforts and the benefits that have accrued to the country through these programmes. The social services from INSAT/GSAT systems in various areas of communication, in addition to the tele-education and tele-medicine continued. Remote sensing application projects continued at national, state and local levels made significant progress. The Disaster Management Support (DMS)

Programme continuing to provide space based inputs for the effective management of disasters in the country. This programme helps in monitoring of natural disasters such as floods, cyclones, landslides, forest fires, etc. In 2017, ISRO supported 29 disasters across 22 counties by providing around 140 sets of IRS data. The Mars Orbiter Mission (MOM), which is India's first inter–planetary spacecraft mission, has successfully completed three years in its orbit around Mars and still continues to provide vital information on regular basis. AstroSat, India's first multi-wavelength observatory, completed two years in orbit. The satellite is now being operated as an 'Observatory', in which observational time is allocated to interested researchers and scientists in the country. (*India, 2020*).

Department of Biotechnology

Another important area in Indian science is Biotechnology which is a set of rapidly emerging and far reaching new technologies with great promises in areas of sustainable food production, nutrition, security, health and environmental sustainability. The GoI, way back in 1982 had set up a multi-agency board namely National Biotechnology Board with the participation of DST, UGC, ICMR and CSIR which was upgraded to a full fledged Department of Biotechnology under the Ministry of Science & Technology in 1986 with the responsibility of administering, development and commercialization in the field of modern biology and biotechnology in India The vision of GoI is to use the powerful tools of biotechnology to help convert the country's diverse biological resources into useful products and processes that are accessible to her masses for economic development and employment generation. For, over the next two decades biotechnology can deliver the next wave of technological change that can be as radical and pervasive as that brought about by IT. The convergence of advances in bio-genomics, proteonics, bioinformatics and IT is drawing the emergence of a new bio-economy. Researches are going on in many specialties like bioinformatics, environmental biotechnology bio-fuels & bio-energy, food & nutrition biotechnology, microfobial & industrial biotechnology, human genetics & genome analysis, bio-engineering, stem cell, medical biotechnology, bio-fertilizers, agricultural biotechnology like bio-fertilizers, bio-pesticides, bio- resources development, medical biotechnology, medicinal & aromatic plants, animal biotechnology, aqua culture & marine biotechnology, seri-biotechnology, etc. etc. A major initiative of the Department has been to develop Stem Cell research in the country and it gave programme support to 6 centres at least. Stem Cell biology is a promising and emerging field of the life sciences. The potential of Stem Cell technology to develop therapy for many untreatable diseases through cellular replacement or tissue engineering is widely recognized. Keeping in view this potential the Department has been supporting a large number of research programmes. The Department has pursued a mission mode programme on bio-fuels and bio-energy. Bioinformatics is another area where the Department has initiated focused development. The BTIS Net Programme of this Department has today developed into an extensive nationwide network covering over 120 institutions spread over the country. The Network provides support to biotechnology research. 52 Bioinformatics facilities were established for introducing innovation in Biology Teaching through Bioinformatics (BTBI). This becomes available to individual institutions as a centralized resource in Bioinformatics research, The Department of Biotechnology has been running a number of autonomous institutions pertaining to areas of its concern, like the Centre for DNA Fingerprinting & Diagnostics, Hyderabad, National Institute of Animal Biotechnology, Hyderabad, National Centre for Cell Science, Pune, National Brain Research Centre, Manesar, Rajiv Gandhi Centre for Biotechnology, Thiruvananathapuram,

Institute of Immunology, Delhi, Institute of Plant Genome Research, Delhi, Institute of Life Science, Bhubaneswar, Institute of Bioresources & Sustainable Development, Imphal, and three public sector undertakings, namely Bharat Immunologicals and Biologicals Corporation Ltd, Bulandshahar, Indian Vaccine Corporation Ltd., Delhi, and Biotech Consortium India Ltd, New Delhi.

DBT has established 16 autonomous institutes for pursuing research in various disciplines of biotechnology in the specialized areas of agriculture and allied sciences, heath care, animal sciences, environment, and industry engaged in the theme-based research with projects sponsored by the national and international agencies. More than 80 technologies have been developed under the efforts of these institutes and many of them have been commercialized through technology transfer. These institutes are the following:

National Institute of Immunology (NII), New Delhi,

National Centre for Cell Sciences (NCCS) Pune,

Centre for DNA Finger printing and Diagnostics (CDFD), Hyderabad,

Institute of Life Sciences (ILS), Bhubaneshwar,

National Brain Research Centre (NBRC), Manesar,

National Institute of Plant Genome Research (NIPGR), Delhi,

Rajiv Gandhi Centre for Biotechnology (RGCB), Thiruvananthapuram,

Institute of Bio-resources and Sustainable Development (IBSD),Imphal,

Centre of Innovative and Applied Bio-processing (CIAB), Mohali,

National Institute of Biomedical Genomics (NIBMG), Kalyani,

Regional Centre for Biotechnology (RCB), Faridabad,

Translational Health Science and Technology Institute (THSTI), Faridabad,

National Institute of Animal Biotechnology (NIAB), Hyderabad,

Institute of Stem Cell Science and Regenerative Medicine (InStem), Bangalauru,.

National Agri Food Biotechnology Cente (NABI), Mohali,

International Centre for Genetic Engineering and Biotechnology (ICGEB), Delhi.

The Department promotes biotech research through the setting up of biotechnology parks, where facilities for technology incubation technology demonstration and pilot plant studies are provided for commercial development of biotechnology. Such parks have been established in different parts of the country to facilitate biotech product development, entrepreneurship, research and innovation in partnership with state and central government organizations, *The Bangalore Life Science Cluster for Muti-scale Basic and Applied Research in Biological Sciences (B-Life), Bangaluru* promotes research and technology development through generation of ideas, sharing resources and infrastructure amongst the partnering institutes, The *NCR Biotech Science Cluster* is established by involving five autonomous institutes of the Department, namely, NIL¸NIPGR, NBRC, THSTI and RCB. The cluster is supporting discovery driven research in biology and development of novel technologies and facilitation of public-private partnerships through biotech business incubators and parks on a network basis. (*India 2020*)

MINISTRY OF EARTH SCIENCES

The Ministry of Earth Science was established in GoI in 2006 by renaming the Ministry of Ocean Development which in turn was the successor to the original Department of Ocean Development established 1981.This was signally a change of perspective of the GoI. Earth Sciences cover a gamut of policies and programmes that contribute to societal benefits in areas of weather, and weather advisories specific to agriculture, aviation, shipping, sports, etc., Monsoon, Disasters (like cyclone, earthquake, tsunami, sea level rise), Living and Non-living resources (like fishery advisory, poly-metallic modules, Gas hydrates, etc.), Coastal and Marine Ecosystems, and Climate Change. The vision of the Ministry is to excel in knowledge and technology enterprises in the realms of the earth system science (including atmosphere, biosphere, hydrosphere, cryosphere and geosphere) towards socio-economic benefit of the Indian subcontinent and in the Indian Ocean region. In the area of Atmospheric Science and Information Services the IMD besides monitoring and forecasting cyclones provides relevant data and advice to members of the World Meteorological Organization (WMO). Similarly, in the areas of monsoon prediction, weather forecasting, early tsunami warnings, integrated coastal and marine area management, climate change studies, etc the respective agencies coming under the purview of the Ministry of Earth Sciences are rendering wonderful services to the people.

Earth System Science Organization (ESSO)

The ESSO having been established in 2007 as a virtual organization, operates as an executive arm of the Ministry of Earth Sciences (MoES) for its policies and programmes. The ESSO brings all meteorological and ocean development activities under one umbrella. It has four major branches of earth sciences, viz, (i) Ocean Science and Technology, (ii) Atmospheric and Climate Science, (iii) Geo-science and Technology, and (iv) Polar Science and Cryo-sphere. The organization is primarily aimed to develop and improve capability to forecast weather, climate and hazard related phenomena for social, economic and environmental benefits including addressing aspects relating to climate change science, and climate services. ESSO is also responsible for development of technology towards the exploration and exploitation of marine resources in a sustainable way for the socio-economic benefit of the society by taking into account the global developments in the field of marine environment. One of the mandates of ESSO is also to promote research in polar science of both Antarctic and Arctic regions to understand the various phenomena and processes of regions on global climate and weather, in particular on the Indian Ocean. ESSO functions through the following centres:

Centre for Marine Living Resources and Ecology (CMLRE), Kochi,

National Centre for Coastal Research (NCCR),

National Centre for Seismology (NCS),

National Centre for Medium Range Weather Forecasting (NCMRWF), Noida,

Indian Meteorological Department (IMD),

National Institute of Ocean Technology (NIOT), Chennai,

Indian National Centre for Ocean Information Services (INCOIS), Hyderabad,

National Centre for Polar and Ocean Research (NCPOR),

Indian Institute of Tropical Meteorology (IITM), Pune, and

National Centre for Earth Sciences Studies (NCESS).

The following activities and programmes of the ESSO are worth special recording: the Atmospheric and Climate Research and weather forecasts; the Agro -Meteorological Advisory Services in collaboration with the Indian Council of Agricultural Research (ICAR), the Global Ensemble Forecast System (GEFS) for Heat and Cold Waves, the Ocean Services, Technology, Observations, Resources Modelling and Science (O-SMART), and the Atmospheric and Climate Research, Observations Science Services (ACROSS).

Department of Ocean Development

The Department of Ocean Development which was originally part of the Ministry of Science & Technology is now functioning as part of the Ministry of Earth Sciences. It is concerned with the Marine Scientific Research in India. Recognizing the necessity of research vessels for conducting Marine Scientific Research, the Department of Ocean Development acquired two state-of-the-art Research Vessels, namely *Sagar Kanya* and *Sagar Sampada* in 1983 and 1984, respectively. These vessels are equipped with advanced scientific instruments to conduct multi-disciplinary research and have contributed in a large way to the advancement of Oceanographic and Atmospheric Research in India for nearly two decades now. So far these vessels have conducted over 230 and 247 cruises respectively in the Indian Ocean for the exploration and exploitation of living and non-living resources including the Antarctic Krill resources. In 1998, two Coastal Research Vessels were also added for monitoring the costal pollution aspects.

Ocean Services: Technology and Observations

The Indian National Centre for Ocean Information Services (INCOIS) provides PFZ advisories to 2.75 lakh fishermen on a daily basis to help them to easily locate the areas of abundant fish in the ocean.

Ocean Forecasts : Ocean state forecasts about waves, currents, sea surface temperature etc. to fisher folk, shipping industry, oil and natural gas industry, navy, coast guard and other stakeholders have improved considerably.

Indian Tsunami Warning System established by the Ministry at the INCOIS has been recognized as the Regional Tsunami Service Provider for the Indian Ocean region by UNESCO to provide warning to countries of the Indian Ocean.

Polar and Cryosphere Research (PACER) : The National Centre for Antarctic and Ocean Research (NCAOR),

Goa established a high altitude research station in Himalayas called *Himarish* situated above 13,500 ft. and is equipped for hydrological balance / modeling, monitoring Glaciers for mass balance, dynamics, energy balance and hydrology.

Seismology & Geoscience Research (SAGE) : The national seismological network consisting 115 observatories has been functioning smoothly. Information pertaining to signifciant earthquake events were transmitted to all concerned state and central government agencies, dealing with relief and rescue operations in the region and also posted on the website.

Research, Education and Training Outreach (REACHOUT) Programme is a scheme that provides support to academic / research organizations in various sectors of earth system sciences including technology development.

MINISTRY OF DEFENCE – THE DRDO

The Defence Research and Development Organization (DRDO) is the Research and Development wing of the GoI .It works under the Department of Defence Research & Development of the Ministry of Defence. It is dedicated towards enhancing self-reliance in Defence Systems and undertakes design and development leading to production of world class weapon systems and equipment in accordance with the expressed needs and the qualitative requirements laid down by the three services, Army, Navy and Air Force. Its vision is to make India prosperous by establishing world class science and technology base and provide our Defence Services decisive edge by equipping them with internationally competitive systems and solutions. DRDO was originally formed in 1958. Then it was a small organization with 10 establishments of laboratories. Over the years it has grown multi-directionally in terms of the variety of subject disciplines, number of laboratories, achievements and stature. Today, DRDO is a network of more than 50 laboratories which are deeply engaged in developing defence technologies covering various disciplines, like aeronautics, armaments, electronics, combat vehicles, engineering systems, instrumentation, missiles, advanced computing and simulation, special materials, naval systems, life sciences, training, information systems, and agriculture. At present the organization is backed by 5,000 scientists and 25,000 scientific, technical and support personnel. Several major projects for the development of missiles, armaments, light combat aircrafts, radars, electronic warfare systems, etc, are on hand and significant achievements have already been made in several such technologies (*www.drdo.gov.in*)..

MINISTRY OF HEALTH & FAMILY WELFARE – THE ICMR

The Indian Council of Medical Research (ICMR) is the continuation of the Indian Research Fund Association set up in 1911 with the specific objective of sponsoring and coordinating medical research in India. In 1949 it was renamed as the Indian Council of Medical Research and is being funded by the GoI through the Department of Health Research of the Ministry of Health & Family Welfare. The Governing Body of the ICMR is presided over by the Union Health Minister. There is a Scientific Advisory Board comprising eminent experts in different biomedical disciplines to assist the ICMR, which in turn is assisted by a series of Scientific Advisory Groups, Committees, Experts, Task Forces, Steering Committees, etc. The Council promotes biomedical research in the country through both intramural and extramural researches. For Intramural Research currently there are 32 Research Institutes/Centes/Units. They include 2 mission oriented National Institutes located in different parts of India, 6 Regional Medical Research Centres, and 5 Units/Centres dealing with various subject areas. In Extramural Research the ICMR promotes the Centres of Advanced Research set up in different research areas in departments of medical colleges and universities. Further Task Force Studies with defined targets are also promoted in multi-centric structures, as well as open ended research through grant-in-aid to scientists in non-ICMR institutes, medical colleges, or universities.

MINISTRY OF EDUCATION (MoE)

The Ministry of Education, formerly the Ministry of Human Resources Development (1985-2020) is responsible for the implementation and formulation of the *National Policy on Education* approved by the Union Cabinet of India and to ensure that it is implemented in letter and spirit. Planned development, including expanding access and improving quality of the educational institutions throughout the country, including in the regions where people do not have easy access to education. The Ministry is further divided into two departments, the Department of School Education and Literacy,which deals with primary, secondary and higher secondary education, adult education and literacy, and the Department of Higher Education, which deals with university; education, technical education, scholarship, etc, (*www.en.em.wikipedia.org*)

Universities are the cradles of innovation and research. When India became independent there were only 20 universities and about 500 colleges. But, at present there are 875 universities and university-level institutions (as on 1 June 2020) of which 54 re central universities, 411 are State Universities, 287 are private universities,123 are Deemed Universities (*www.en.em.wikipedia.org.wiki:list of...*), and more than 38,000 colleges. Besides, there are 33 institutions of national importance established under Acts of Parliament, and 5 institutions established under various State legislations. Besides engaging in direct teaching, University departments are catering to basic and fundamental research leading to award of Ph.D. degrees, and the quality and competence of teachers and departments are often measured in terms of the number of research degrees produced by them.

GoI by an Act of the Parliament had constituted the University Grants Commission (UGC) in 1953 as the national body for the coordination, determination and maintenance of standards of university education. It served as a coordinating body between the Union and State Governments and the institutions of higher learning. It also acted as an advisory body to these Governments and institutions on issues relating to higher education. UGC had its headquarters in New Delhi but it has later decentralized its operations by setting up Regional Centres at Pune, Hyderabad, Kolkotta, Bhopal, Guwahati and Bangaluru. The Commission provided financial assistance also by allocating and disbursing funds provided by the GoI as grants to universities and colleges for their maintenance and development. UGC established the National Assessment and Accreditation Council (NAAC) in 1994 at Bangaluru for doing performance evaluation, assessment and accreditation of the universities and colleges. The system of NAAC Accreditation administered by the UGC has led to substantial qualitative improvement in higher education and research in the country as a whole. The Modi governemrnt has announced that it will dissolve the UGC and replace it with a new Higher Education Commission of India (HECI). This will be the new ,apex regulator for university and higher education in India, It has to set benchmarks for academic performance, ensure that institutions adhere to these and act against those that violate standards. It will replace the UGC once the Parliament repeals UGC Act 1951. The HECI will then be governed by a Commission headed by a Chairperson and a Vice Chairperson who are selected by a Committee which will include the Cabinet Secretary and the Higher Education Secretary (*m.economictimes. com* delivered by Google, downloaded on 26/09/2020)..

MINISTRY OF AGRICULTURE - AGRICULTURAL UNIVERSITIES & ICAR

The Indian Council of Agricultural Research (ICAR) was originally established in 1929 as a registered society under the Societies Registration Act, 1860. After independence, the Department of Agricultural Research & Education (DARE) under the Ministry of Agriculture, GoI, provided government support to the ICAR by making it an apex body at the national level responsible for coordinating research and educational activities in the field of agriculture, animal husbandry and fisheries. ICAR is an autonomous body. DARE has one more autonomous body, namely the Central Agricultural University at Imphal. But, ICAR is a robust body with headquarters in New Delhi and with a vast network of institutions all over the country, consisting of 49 Institutes including National Institutes having Deemed University status, 6 National Bureaus, 17 National Research Centres, 25 Project Directorates, 61 All India Coordinated Research Projects (AICRP), including 17 Network Projects and 607 Krishi Vikas Kendras. For higher education in agriculture and allied fields there are 56 State Agricultural Universities and one Central Agricultural University. With an extensive research network of research infrastructure, backed by excellent team of scientists and other personnel the ICAR is making rapid strides in agricultural research and provides support to the national efforts in achieving food security and self-sufficiency. Both research and higher education are facilitated in subject areas like: Crop Sciences, Horticulture, Natural Resources Management, Agricultural Engineering, Animal Sciences, Fisheries, Agricultural Education, and Agricultural Extension. ICAR also maintains a Directorate of Knowledge Management in Agriculture. ICAR played a pivotal role in ushering the era of green and yellow revolutions in the country. ICAR helped to increase the production of food grains by 4 times, horticultural crop by 6 times, fish by 9 times (marine 5 times and in land 17 times), and milk by 6 times.

MINISTRY OF ENVIRONMENT, FORESTS & CLIMATE CHANGE (MoEFCC)

MoEFCC is the nodal agency in the administrative structure of the Central Government for planning, promotion, co-ordination and overseeing the implementation of India's environmental and forestry policies and programmes, The Ministry was named the Ministry of Environment and Forests until 2014 when it was renamed to the current title (*Economic Times, 28 May 2014*). The broad objectives of the Ministry are: Conservation and survey of flora, fauna, forests and wildlife; Prevention and control of pollution; Afforestation and Land degradation; Protection of the environment; and Ensuring the Welfare of animals, These objectives are supported by various legislative and regulative measurers, and through formulation of relevant national policies and programmes.

The Botanical Survey of India (BSI)

The BSI is the apex research organization under the Ministry of Environment, Forest, and Climate Change for carrying out the taxonomic and floristic studies on wild plant resources of the country. BSI was established in 1890 in Kolkata with the basic objective of exploring, collecting, identifying and documenting the plant resources of the country, and identifying the plant species with economic virtues. After independence, BSI was reorganized in 1954 by GoI. During the successive Plan periods the functions of the BSI were expanded to include various new areas, such as inventorying of endemic, rare and threatened species, evolving conservation strategies, studies on fragile ecosystems and protected areas, like wildlife sanctuaries, natural parks and biosphere reserves, multiplication and maintenance of endemic and threatened plant species, wild ornamentals, etc. With its headquarters at the Central National Herbarium, Central Botanical Laboratory, main Garden at Howrah, the Botanical Museum at Calcutta the BSI has nine regional circles or stations in different parts of the country, namely Dehradun, Coimbatore,

Shillong, Pune, Allahabad, Jodhpur, Port Blair, Gangtok and New Itanagar. These stations have regional herbaria with about 2,000,000 specimens; nearly 250 new plants (genera and species) have so far been discovered and described while more than 500 new records of plants have been found for our country. The *Flora of India* with its national and state volumes is the prestigious publication of BSI.(*www.biologydiscussion.com* downloaded on 29/09/2020).

The Zoological Survey of India (ZSI)

The ZSI is presently a part of the Ministry of Environment, Forest and Climate Change. The ZSI since its inception in 1916 with Headquarters at Kolkata and 16 Regional stations located in different parts of the country, has been undertaking survey, exploration and research leading to the advancement of our knowledge on the exceptionally rich faunal diversity of India. In recent years ZSI has reorganized its work by grouping the survey and studies under six major programmes, namely Study of Fauna of States; Fauna of Conservation areas; Fauna of Important Ecosystems; Status survey of endangered species; Fauna of India and Ecological Studies /Environment Impact Assessment Survey; and Identification of Wildlife Seized material related to Wildlife (Protection) Act, 1972, etc. The ZSI had acquired the zoological collections of more than a century old from the former museum of the Asiatic Society of Bengal and the zoological section of the Indian Museum (1814-1875) in Calcutta. A total of 15,532 specimens including 789 Aves (observed) and 234 Mammals (sighted) under 18 faunal groups were collected, of which 558 species were of 12 faunal groups. The Library of the ZSI which was functioning from 1949 to 2000 in the Indian Museum, was transferred to the New Annexed Building of ZSI at New Alipur in 2000. The library holdings both at the Headquarter Library, Kolkata and the 16 Regional Centres located in different parts of India have a total collection of approximately; 135,519 documents, which includes books, bound and unbound journals, monographs, reports of expeditions and faunal surveys, non-book materials etc, Among the publications of ZSI the most significant ones are the *Fauna of India* and the *State Fauna Series* (20 states). (*en.m.wikipedia.org-Zoological Survey of India* downloaded on 29/09/2020).

The Forest Survey of India (FSI)

The FSI was founded in 1981 with its headquarters at Dehra Dun, Uttarakhand, and four Regional Offices at Shimla, Kolkata, Nagpur, and Bangaluru is a premier national organization for forest resource assessment, collection of data on scientific lines through country wide comprehensive forest resources surveys at regular intervals, coming under the Ministry of Environment, Forest and Climate Change. FSI is virtually the successor of the "Parliament Survey of Forest Resources", a project initiated in 1965 by the GoI with the sponsorship of the Food and Agricultural Organization and the United Nations Development Programme. FSI in Dehra Dun, besides administrative and technical control, is mainly engaged in forest cover mapping data processing and in conducting trainings. The Regional Offices are mainly engaged in inventory of forests and trees outside forests. Since 2004 FSI has been monitoring forest fires across the country using MODIS (Moderate–Resolution Imaging Spectrometer) and GIS based technology (*en.m.wikipedia.org/Forest Survey of India* downloaded on 29/09/2020).

Environmental Research

The Ministry with its Research and Development programme under a Central Plan Scheme since 1985 has been continuously funding research in multi-disciplinary aspects of environmental and ecosystems protection, conservation and management at various universities, institutions of higher learning, national research institutes and non-governmental organizations in identified thrust areas. The objectives of the scheme are to generate information required for developing strategies, technologies and methodologies for better environmental management. The Ministry supports research through its established research programmes, like Environmental Research Programme (ERP), Ecosystem Research Schemes (ERS), Eastern & Western Ghats Research Programme (E&WGRP), etc. It also gives Awards of National Fellowships to outstanding scientists. Besides the work of National Natural Resources Management System, other programmes of research like those on Wetlands, Mangroves and Coral Reefs, Forestry, Wildlife, etc, are being carried on. The Ministry has set up 10 Centres of Excellence with a view to strengthening awareness, research and training in priority areas of environmental science and management. The G. B. Pant Institute of Himalayan Environment and Development at Almora was established by the Ministry in 1988. The Indian Council of Forestry Research and Education (ICFRE) was created as an apex body in the national forestry research system. Above all must be mentioned that the Ministry has set up the Environmental Information System (ENVIS) as a comprehensive network in environmental information for the collection, collation, storage, retrieval and dissemination to the varying users. ENVIS now consists 76 network partners out of which 48 are subject specific while 36 are State related. In 2019 the GoI has signed an MoU with the University of British Columbia, Canada to work on various environmental issues including climate change, forest resource management and wildlife. This pact will be for next 10 years to explore opportunities for collaboration in the fields of forestry science, through organizations like Indian Council of Forestry Research and Education (ICFRE), Wildlife Institute of India (WII), Forest Survey of India (FSI), Indira Gandhi National Forest Academy and Directorate of Forest Education, Uttarakhand, and UBC. (*www. currentaffairs, gktoday.in* down loaded on 29/09/2020).

MINISTRY OF COMMUNICATIONS

The former Ministry of Communication and Information Technolgoy was bifurcated into Ministry of Communications and Ministry of Electronics and Information Technology in July 2016. There are two departments coming under the Ministry of Communications. They are the Department of Posts, and the Department of Telecommunication.

Department of Posts (DOP)

For more than 150 years, the DOP has been the backbone of the country's communication and has played a crucial role in the country's social and economic development. It touches the lives of Indian citizens in many ways: delivering mails, accepting deposits under Small Savings Schemes, providing life insurance cover under Postal Life Insurance and Rural Postal Life Insurance and providing retail services like bill collection, sale of forms, etc. The DoP also acts as an agent for GoI in discharging other services for citizens such as Mahatma Gandhi National Rural Employment Guarantee Scheme, wage disbursement and old age pension payments. India has the largest postal network in the world with 155,531 post offices as on 22-09-2020 (*www.indiapost.gov.in* downloaded on 30/09/2020), of which almost 90% are in rural areas. At the time of independence, there were 23,344 post offices which were primarily in urban areas. The network has registered a sevenfold growth since independence. Currently this is the most widely distributed post office system in the world (*en.m.wikipedia.org* downloaded on 01/10/2020).

Indian postal system is seeking a paradigm shift to become a technology enabled organization. The key initiatives in this direction are technology induction programmes like computerization & networking of the existing post offices, transforming them into a state of the art electronic network for improving service delivery, and introduction of various new services like e-posts, e-bill posts, e-money orders, instant money orders, international money transfer service, etc. The GOI had set up the Telecom Commission in 1989 with the major functions of policy formulation, review of performance, licensing, wireless spectrum management, administrative monitoring, standardization, validation of equipment and international relations. Research and development in matters relating to the Indian postal system is also a major function of the Commission. The Centre for Excellence in Postal Technology (CEPT), Mysore was developed by the DOP to attend to its technology needs. The Cabinet Committee on Economic Affairs approved IT modernization project of DOP in November 2012, with a total outlay of Rs 4,909 crores. One of the key objectives of the project was the modernization and computerization of all post offices in the country to provide better customer service and IT enablement of business processes and support functions. The entire project was implemented by the department. (ET Government, February 17, 2020, *government.economictimes, indiatimes.com* downloaded on 01/10/2020).

Department of Telecommunication (DOT)

GOI recognizes that provision of world class telecommunications infrastructure and information is the key to rapid economic and social development of the country. Accordingly, the GOI set up the Telecom Commission in 1989 with the administrative and financial powers of the GOI to deal with various aspects of telecommunications. The National Telecom Policy was announced in 1994 which was revised in 1999. The Telecom Regulatory Authority in India (TRAI) was established in 1997. The Department of Telecommunication (DOT) is now responsible for policy formulations, performance review, monitoring, international cooperation, research & development, etc. C-Dot, an autonomous society under DOT is carrying out research & development for areas of national importance in Telecommunication, and is working on various developmental projects like a shared Global System of Mobile Communication Radio Access Network for rural India. The ITI Limited is India's pioneering venture in the field of telecommunications since 1948 with state-of-the-art manufacturing facilities spread across 6 locations and a countrywide network of marketing and service outlets. In 1978 the GOI had established the Telecommunications Consultants India Ltd (TCIL) with the objective of extending the wide ranging Indian telecom expertise to friendly developing countries. The Company has since then been engaged in adopting world class communication and IT technologies for catering to the total needs of countries mainly in the developing world. The Department has been formulating developmental policies for the accelerated growth of the telecommunication services In August 2020 the Prime Minster has inaugurated the Submarine Optical Fibre Cable connectivity between Chennai and Andaman and Nicobar Islands (*www.dot.gov.in* downloaded on 01/10/2020).

MINISTRY OF ELECTRONICS AND INFORMATION TECHNOLGY (MeitY)

Previously known as the Department of Information Technology, it was renamed as the Department of Electronics and Information Technology in 2012. On 19th July 2016 this was made into a full fledged ministry which henceforth is known as the Ministry of Electronics and Information Technology (MeitY), bifurcating it from the Ministry of Communication and Information Technology.

Department of Information Technology (DIT)

The DIT is *inter alia* responsible for policy formulation, performance, review, monitoring, international co-operation, grant of licenses to operators for providing basic and value added services as per the approved policy of GOI. All policy matters relating to silicon facility, computer based information technology and processing, including hardware and software, standardization of procedures and matters relating to e-commerce, internet, information technology education, and development of electronics and coordination amongst its various users are dealt with by the DIT. Among the various initiatives of the DIT, the National e-Governance Plan, the State Wide Area Networks scheme, the establishment of Broadband Internet Enabled Common Service Centres (CSCs), the State Data Centres (SDCs) scheme, the Cyber Security oriented R&D initiatives, the Technology Development for Indian Languages, Nanotechnology and Micro-electronics, Human Resource Development, National Knowledge Network (NKN), etc. are among the many that are worth mentioning. Indian IT industry is now a global IT hub. There is urgent need for strengthening R&D institutions and R&D resources to meet the demand of IT and electronics industry. The Centre for Development of Advanced Computing (C-DAC) is a premier R&D organization under the DIT. It has network of laboratories across the country and its focus areas are technologies of great relevance to the nation. At present there are 6 thematic areas of focus in C-DAC, namely, High Performance Computing and Grid Computing, Multilingual Computing, Professional Electronics including VLSI and Embedded Systems, Software Technologies including FOSS, Cyber Security and Cyber Forensics, and Health Informatics. The DOEACC Society is an autonomous Scientific Society of DIT to carry out human resource development and related activities in the area of Information, Electronics and Communication Technology. The Society has its centres in all important cities in the country. These centres are offering consultancy services and undertaking software development projects in addition to Government sponsored projects in the area of Education & Training, R&D, etc. The Software Technology Parks of India (STPI) was set up in 1991 by DIT with the main objective of promoting software exports from the country. The Centre for Materials for Electronics Technology (C-MET) at Pune, Hyderabad and Thrissur, are engaged in developing the knowledge base in Electronics materials and their processing technologies for Indian industries. The Society for Applied Microwave Electronics Engineering and Research (SAMEER) is an autonomous R&D Laboratory under DIT working for the development of data communication systems to enhance the quality and security of information transfer. The National Informatics Centre (NIC) is a premier S&T organization of DIT, established in 1976, which has been providing informatics support to Central Ministries, State Governments, and District Administrations for the last few decades. It has extended its ICT support to a few neighbouring countries also. A country wide satellite based communication network, NICNET, has been set up as backbone network infrastructure for Government informatics providing linkages in 36 States/ Union Territories and 708 districts. The network infrastructure links over 3,000 nodes in Wide Area Network and about 50,000 nodes of Local Areas Network operations facility across the country. A wide range of services are provided through NIC including Web Services, Messaging Services, e-Commerce, e-Learning, Office Automation, IT Consultancy Services, Digital Archiving, Geographic Information Systems, Utility Mapping, Computer Aided Design, training, etc. In 2018, NIC opened its fourth data centre in Bhubaneshwar to complement its existing data centres in New Delhi, Hyderabad and Pune. In May 2019, the GOI set up the Centre for Smart Governance (CSG), and state governments have since been advised to consult the CSG for IT projects they previously would have consulted the NIC and private firms for. (*en.em.wikipedia.org* downloaded on 01/10/2020).

SCIENCE & TECHNOLGOY INSTITUTIONS IN THE STATE OF KERALA

Thiruvananthapuram district

A B J Abdul Kalam Technological University, Trivandrum

Achuta Menon Centre for Health Sciences Studies, Medical

College

Centre for Development of Advanced Computing (C-DAC), Vellayambalam.

Centre for Mathematical and Statistical Sciences, Trivandrum.

College of Agriculture (Kerala Agricultural University), Vellayani

College of Engineering, Trivandrum (CET), Sreekaryam.

CSIR- National Institute for Interdisciplinary Science and Technology, Pappanamcode,

Govt. Ayurveda College, Trivandrum.

Govt. Medical College, Trivandrum

Govt. Medical College, Trivandrum, Multi-disciplinary Research Unit (MRU)

Hindustan Latex, Trivandrum (Peroorkada & Poojappura).

ICAR-Central Tuber Crops Research Institute, Sreekaryam.

Indian Institute of Space Science and Technology (IIST), Valiamala

Indian Institute of Information Technology and Management, Teknopark.

ISRO-Indian Institute of Science Education and Research, Trivandrum

ISRO- Inertial System Unit (IISU), Vattiyoorkavu.

ISRO- Liquid Propulsion System Centre (LPSC), Valiamala.

ISRO- The Vikram Sara Bhai Space Centre (VSSC), Kochu Veli.

Kerala State Industrial Development Centre (KSIDC), Vellayambalam.

KSCSTE – International Institute of Advanced Virology; (IAV), Thirumala & Thonnakkal.

KSCSTE–Jawaharlal Nehru Tropical Botanical Garden and Research Institute, (JNTBGRI), Palode.

KSCSTE-National Transportation Planning and Research Centre, (NATPAC)

L B S Centre, Palayam

Multi disciplinary Research Unit (MRU). Govt, Medical College, Trivandrum.

National Centre for Earth Science Studies (CESS) , Aakkulakm

National Informatics Centre - Kerala State Centre, Vellayambalam

National Institute of Speech and Hearing (NISH), Aakkulam

Orisya Academy of Skill Development and Research, Chavadimukku.

Rajiv Gandhi Centre for Biotechnology (RGCB), Poojapura & Aakkulam

Regional Cancer Centre, Medical College

Sree Chitra Tirunal Institute for Medical Sciences & Technology, Medical College

Sree Chitra Tirunal Institute for Medical Sciences & Technology, Bio Medical Technology Wing, Poojapura.

Kollam district

Central Plantation Crops Research Institute, Krishnapuram

Corporate Research Centre, Indian Rare Earths Ltd,, Kollam.

ICAR-Coconut Research Centre, Kayamkulam.

Onattukara Regional Agricultural Research Station, Kayamkulam.

Alapuzha district

Central Coir Research and Innovation, Alapuzha

National Institute of Virology (NIV), Kerala Unit, Vandanam.

Regional Agricultural Research Station, Kumarakom.

Rice Research Station, Moncompu

Pathanamthitta district

Kerala Agricultural University - Agricultural Research Station, Tiruvalla

Pushpagiri Institute of Medical Sciences and Research Centre, Tiruvalla

Pushpagiri Centre for Virology, Tiruvalla

Idukki district

Biofarms Research and Development Centre, Ramakkalmedu.

Horti Research Centre, Chettukuzhi

Indian Cardamom Research Institute, Mailadumkunnu

Pineapple Research Station, Muvattupuzha.

Kottayam district

Centre for Mathematical and Statistical Sciences, Pala

Govt. Medical College, Kottayam.

ICMR- Vector Control Research Centre (VCRC), Kottayam.

Mahatma Gandhi University, Kottayam.

Rubber Research Institute of India, Kottayam.

Ernakulam district

Advanced Centre for Atmospheric Radar Research, Ernakulam.

Amrita Institute of Medical Sciences and Research, Ponekkara.

Cochin Shipyard, Perumanoor.

Centre for Marine Living Resources and Ecology (CMLRE), (Ministry of Earth Sciences), LNG Road, Ernakulam.

Central Institute of Fisheries Technology (CIFT), Mattancherry.

Cochin Cancer Research Centre, Ernakulam.

CIPET Centre for Biopolymer Science and Technology, Ernakulam

Central Marine Fisheries Research Institute (CMFRI), Ernakulam.

Cochin University of Science and Technology (CUSAT), Kalamassery.

CSIR- National Institute of Oceanography, Ernakulam.

KAU- Rice Research Centre, Ernakulam.

Keltron Toolroom Research and Training Centre (KELTRAC), Aroor.

Kerala University of Fisheries and Ocean Studies, (KUFOS), Panangad

Nansen Environmental Research Centre (India), Ernakulam.

National Centre for Aquatic Animal Health(NCAAH), CUSAT Department, Ernakulam.

National Physical & Oceanographic Laboratory (NPOL), Ernakulam.

Thrissur district

Academy of Climate Change Education and Research, (KAU), Thrissur.

Agronomic Research Station, Chalakudy.

Amala Cancer Hospital and Research Centre, Thrissur

Banana Research Station, State Dept of Agriculture, Panachery

Cashew Research Station, Madakkathara

College of Forestry (Kerala Agricultural University), Vellanikkara

College of Horticulture, (Kerala Agricultural University), Vellanikkara

Jawaharlal Nehru Botanical Research Centre, Kakkulissery.

Jubilee Centre for Medical Research (JCMR), Thrissur.

Kaps Research Centre, Thrissur.

Kerala Agricultural University (KAU), Vellanikkara.

Kerala Forest Research Institute (KVASU), Peechi.

Kerala Engineering Research Institute, Peechi.

Kerala Veterinary and Animal Sciences University, Mannuthy.

Regional Agricultural Research Station, Pattambi.

River Research Centre, Thrissur

Water Management and Research Unit (Kerala Agricultural University),Thrissur..

Palakkad district

Indian Institute of Technology, Palakkad (IIT-P), Kanjikode.

Institute of Integrative Medical Sciences, Govt. Medical College, Palakkad.

IRTC- Integrated Rural Technology Centre, Mundur,

Malappuram distrtict

University of Calicut, Thenjipalam.

KSCSTE-Kerala Forest Research Institute (KFRI), Sub-Centre, Nilambur.

Kelappaji College of Agricultural Engineering & Technology, Thavanur.

Govt. Medical College, Kozhikode.

ICAR- Central Marine Fisheries Research Institute, Calicut Research Centre, West Hill.

ICAR- Indian institute of Spices Research (IISR), Vellimadukunnu.

Indian Institute of Management –Kozhikode (IIM-K), Kunnamangalam.

KSCSTE- Kerala School of Mathematics, (KSoM), Kunnamangalam,

KSCSTE- The Malabar Botanical Garden & Institute of Plant Sciences (MBGIPS),

National Institute of Technology, Calicut (NITC),

Zoological Survey of India (ZSI), Western Ghats Research Centre, (WGRC), Calicut.

Kannur district

Kannur University,

Pepper Research Station, (Kerala Agriculural University) Payyannur

Malabar Cancer Centre, Thalassery.

Wayanad district

M.S. Swaminathan Research Foundation-Community Agro-Biodiversity Centre, Meppadi.

Kasargode district

Central University of Kerala, Kasargode

ICAR –Central Plantation Crops Research institute, Kasargode.

KAU-Pepper Research Station, Payyannur, Kerala Agricultural University

SCIENCE INFORMATION SYSTEM SET UP IN INDIA

In this section you are going to be introduced to a remarkable model of a nation-wide science and technology information systems which was once developed in India. This is none other than the NISSAT. Although NISSAT had to be dropped out of the national budget of the Government of India after the financial year 2002-03 the infrastructure that came to be established and made operational in the country still continues to serve the objectives for which it was originally established.

Background of NISSAT

Almost every science institution in India had its own information system set up, either big or small, like a library, information centre, or documentation centre, which operates varying ranges of services to its parent institution and its clientele. The first time an effort was made to coordinate and develop these existing and independent services was during the time when the Fifth Five Year Plan proposals were formulated. This was also the first time that a Five Year Plan ever contained a Science and Technology Plan. The Science & Technology Plan gave proposals for the development of a National Information System for Science and Technology during the Fifth Five Year Plan period. It was a clear evidence of the recognition given by the Government and policy makers to the role of information, and S & T information particularly, in the social and economic development of the country, and the realization that information is an instrument of social change. It was hoped that NISSAT when fully developed would enable the country to meet all the information demands of all types of users.

When the NISSAT was proposed there were about 1,000 information centres in India covering the various field of S & T, with differing functions, scope and efficiency, scattered among a large number of science agencies, research laboratories, universities, institutes of higher learning, professional colleges, professional associations, government departments, public and private sector industries and R & D organizations. The information facilities in these centres were intended to meet the local needs of scientists, engineers, research workers, technicians, policy makers, industrialists, etc. These institutions, being independent units, cannot be self reliant because of the continuously expanding scientific knowledge, the growing specialization of science, and the increasingly multi-disciplinary nature of S&T.

NISSAT Proposals

NISSAT envisaged

1. Interlinking and coordination of the existing and future scientific and technical information sources, systems, and services into an organized and effective network under an overall coordinating agency with a national information policy for its guidance;

2. Identifying lacunae (existing gaps) in information sources, tools and services and initiating efforts to fill up these gaps;
3. Introducing modern information technology and management methods wherever they would improve the efficiency and effectiveness of services;
4. Facilitating inter-change of information by developing and applying inter nationally compatible national standards and guidance for information handling; and
5. Taking advantage of the international programmes by participating in international information systems like the UNISIST.

NISSAT Structure

When the NISSAT was finally established it had the following structure (see chart below):

NISSAT Advisory Committee	Network of Services
• Executive & Ad hoc	National Information Centres (NICs)
• Working Groups	Sectoral Information Centres (SICs)
• Expert Groups	Regional Information Centres (RICs)
• SECRETARIAT	Local Information Units (LIUs)

Fig. 3.2. Chart showing The Nissat Structure

(a) The Department of Science & Technology (DST) will act as **the National Focal Point of NISSAT**. Among other things the DST will be responsible for:
   - the formulation of national STI policy and a national plan of action,
   - establishing mechanisms for implementing the policy and plans,
   - allocating finance for STI programmes,
   - development of information sources and services,
   - development of manpower, and equipment

enumeration" and representing all integrals using 9 digits and a symbol for zero. This dates back to the Vedic period. During the same period Pythagorean geometry was developed. However, the more systematic development for Indian Mathematics dates from Aryabhatta (15th cy AD) who developed techniques for extracting square roots and cube roots.

Indian Medicine, Biology and Agriculture

The Indian Medical knowledge and surgical practices were known to the Asiatic world and the South-East Asia, Tibet and China. The classics of Charaka, Susruta, Madhwa and Vagabhatta were translated into Asian languages by caliphs during the 9th and 10th centuries A.D., and into Latin by Moses Farachi in the 13th cy AD. These became in fact the standard medical compendium of the middles ages.

In Biology Indians had appreciable knowledge of histology, physiology, pathology and reproduction of various plants, besides their systematic classification. The medieval period witnessed the introduction of new plants into India, especially by the Mughals and the Portuguese, like Tobacco, Pineapple, Chillies, Coffee, etc. The Mughals encouraged horticulture, fostered the grafting techniques, especially in mango varieties. The Vedic period and succeeding centuries witnessed new trends in agriculture, like rotation of crops and cultivation of rice.

Indian Crafts, Industry and Technology

Similarly, during the post Vedic centuries there were new trends in industry and craftsmanship, like in metal, wood, leather, textiles, ceramics, jewelry, etc. and the technology of making agricultural implements like plough were in use. India was noted specially for iron metallurgy; the Iron Pillar at Delhi was of the 5th century AD. The advent of paper in the 12th and 13th centuries, possibly from Central Asia might have needed for the services, and

- coordination of the activities in areas of STI.

(b) At the top level of the network will be the present and proposed **National Information Centres (NICs)**. They will be responsible for: coordinating, organizing and providing information services at the national level. A number of major institutions have been designated as NICs, like the INSDOC, the DESIDOC, the BARC, the National Medical Library, the National Agricultural Documentation Centre and Library, the Standards Information Centre and Library of the Bureau of Indian Standards, etc.

(c) All the major S&T areas will be classified into Sectors based on disciplines, missions, products, etc. **Sectoral Information Centres (SICs)** are expected to coordinate its activities with those of the Local Information Units (LIUs) in that particular Sector. An SIC will be generally the part of a National Research Laboratory doing R&D work in the particular discipline, mission or product so that the services of subject specialists could be readily available to the SICs for abstracting, information analysis, etc, and there will be better utilization of the information facilities and products created SICs. SICs are usually built around the existing information resources and facilities by upgrading the same to provide services at national level by augmenting its services and facilities with the financial support of NISSAT. NISSAT has already established several SICs at the national level, like the National Information Centre for Leather Technology, in CLRI Chennai, NIC for Drugs and Pharmaceuticals at the Central Drugs Research Institute, Lucknow, the NIC for Crystallography at the University of Madras, Chennai, etc., about 12 of them until 1997.

(d) **The Local Information Units (LIUs)** are continuing to form part of individual R&D establishments, government departments, industrial enterprises or business firms serving the needs of users in their own institution. LIUs are at the lowest level of NISSAT set up. The users of these LIUs will be the ultimate recipients of information from the NICs and SICs.

(e) **The Regional Information Centres (RICs)**, unlike NICs and SICs, are multidisciplinary centres to act as the NISSAT contact points in each geographical area of R&D, educational, or industrial activity.

NISSAT did not envisage creation of altogether a new set of systems. On the other hand its planned strategy was to make the maximum use of the available infrastructure and resources base. NISSAT as a scheme was not included as a component of the Tenth Five Year Plan by the Planning Commission and finally NISSAT came to an end. Though it has not been possible to provide financial assistance to many of the projects under NISSAT from 2002-03, most of them continued their activities and provided services.

NISSAT Achievements

Although NISSAT programme has been finally wound up by the GoI and DST, the network of libraries and information systems created under the aegis of NISSAT is fully existing and operational. The value of this NISSAT programme as a good model of a national science and technology information system is almost unquestionable.

NISSAT was originally launched in 1977 and it was closed down as a Government supported scheme in 2003. In the course of these 25 years it had tremendous growth and achievements. In tune with the changing global scenario and in pursuance of the national efforts in liberalization and globalization of the economy, NISSAT reoriented its programmes and activities continually in order to be useful to a wider base of clientele in diverse subjects. NISSAT could establish 14 NICs on specific sectors like Leather Technology, Drugs and Pharmaceuticals, Food Technology, Machine Tools Production and Engineering, Textiles and Allied Subjects, Chemicals and Allied Industries, Advanced Ceramics, Crystallography, Bibliometrics, CD-ROMs, Management Sciences, Marine & Aquatic Sciences, Publications on CD-ROMs, and Tea Manufacturing and Marketing. These NICs maintain extensive collections of published and unpublished documents in the form of books, periodicals, R&D reports, Technical reports, Standards, Patents, and Trade literature in their subject areas. Although NISSAT has ceased to give financial support to these centres their services are still maintained by the parent institutions.

NISSAT has established 11 NACIDS (**National Access Centres of International Databases Services)** in Ahmedabad, Bangalore, Calcutta, Chennai, Delhi. Hyderabad, Mumbai, Pune, Thiruvananthapuram, Guwahati, and Bhopal for providing online facility to access international database services. Many of the services operated by the NISSAT, especially its web-based activities, Databases development activities, Information Resources Sharing, and Development of IT skills, etc. have went a long way in establishing India as a country with a strong S&T information system and network.

NISSAT developed a CD-ROM National Collection Centre with CD-ROM databases on India and CD-ROM products produced in India, The Centre was set up at Foundations for Innovations and Technology Transfer in Indian Institute of Technology, Delhi in 1996. The Centre rendered services form CD-ROM collection. This centre has stopped function since 2003.

NISSAT helped establishment of regional networks like DELNET, CALIBNET, BONET, PUNENET, ADINET and MYLIBNE and established the Indian Ocean Server at NIO, Goa, Indian Consultancy Website at DDC, New Delhi,

"Vigyan" an Indian S&T website, and a discussion form called 'LISFORUM' with NSCI at Indian Institute of Science, Bangalore.

NISSAT promoted the use of Standards with training in CCF (Common Communication Format) to earn the status of a *de facto* national standard for exchange of information, creation of databases, etc.

NISSAT promoted Information Technology Applications: NISSAT acquired two software packages namely CDS/ISIS (for bibliographical processing and retrieval) and IDAMS (for statistical data processing) from UNESCO for distribution to Indian institutions. NISSAT in collaboration with DESIDOC developed a software package SANJAY, for automation of house-keeping and service functions of libraries.

NISSAT published a quarterly newsletter, *NISSAT Newsletter* (the title was changed to *Information Today & Tomorrow*, which was suspended in 2002.

REFERENCES

INDIA, Research, Reference and Training Division (2011), *India 2011, A Reference Annual.Edn.55* NewDelhi, Publications Division, 2011..

INDIA, Research, Reference and Training Division (2020), *India 2020, A Reference Annual*. NewDelhi, Publications Division, 2020..

NEELAMEGHAN, A. and PRASAD, K.N. Eds.(1998), *Information systems, networks and services: developments and trends* 2 vols. Bangalore, Institute of Information Studies,1998.

LAHIRI, Abhijit, et al (1998), 'National Information System for Science and Technology (NISSAT)' in Neelameghan, and Prasad, *ibid* Ch.14, pp.221-246.

en.m.economictimes.com delivered by Google, downloaded on 26/09/2020)..

en.em.wikipedia.org downloaded on 01/10/2020

en.m.wikipedia.org/Forest Survey of India downloaded on 29/09/2020.

en.m.wikipedia.org-Zoological Survey of India downloaded on 29/09/2020.

en.m.economictimes.com delivered by Google, downloaded on 26/09/2020..

www.anusandhan.net

www.biologydiscussion.com downloaded on 29/09/2020.

www.currentaffairs,gktoday.in down loaded on 29/09/2020.

www.dot.gov.in downloaded on 01/10/2020.

www.drdo.gov.in..

www.en.em.wikipedia.org.wiki:list of...

*www.government.economictimes,indiatimes.co*m downloaded on 01/10/2020.

www.indiapost.gov.in downloaded on 30/09/2020,

4

Planning of The Science Information Systems

NEED FOR PLANNING

Most librarians and Information professionals will agree that planning is an essential pre-requisite to effective library operations and services. It is doubtful that many of our libraries and information systems had the advantage of good planning. Planning presupposes that the goals and objectives of the system are properly formulated and documented. In the absence of that process, a pattern already got established will go on without any review. More often people go by traditions without venturing into changed conceptions and practices. Many are governed by the axiom that '*the past determines the present and the present foretells the future*'. It is true that the society as a whole is changing as are the social institutions. Library is one such institution which has been containing continuous changes, say in the matter of its philosophy, materials, techniques and even technology. If change is to be significant planning of libraries and information systems must be based on finding answers to the following questions:

- Is the present pattern of our library service the best possible for the future?

- Is it efficient to meet the pressing needs of our clientele?
- Does it consider also the other sources of information available to our clientele?
- Do the priorities of services of our library match with the needs of the clientele?
- Within constraints of time and money, are we providing the most effective library and information service possible?

Planning is a continuous activity in the management of all institutions including a library or information centre. It is an on-going basic management activity. Planning is concerned with the future, like sketching out things that have to happen during the period specified. In that way it is an attempt to bridge the gap between the present and the future. "*Planning is deciding in advance what to do? How to do it? When to do it?, and Who is to do it?*". In other words, planning aims at making certain things happen which otherwise would not have happened in that manner.

ADVANTAGES OF PLANNING

The concept of planning has acquired much discredit among librarians / information scientists primarily because the frequent failures due to unrealistic planning mainly in the government sector. But planning has many positive sides. Without planning most libraries and information centres would have remained poorly organized and ill-equipped to meet the goals and objectives of their parent institutions, and the varied needs of their user communities. On the other hand, planning gives them the overall direction to growth, and minimizes ad hoc decisions in respect of services to be provided. Planning helps:

- in achieving the goals of the institution and the society of which it is a part;
- in identifying and differentiating priority actions,

- in developing concentrated and cohesive actions towards achieving the goals;
- in rechecking, error identifying, and modifying the programmes as and when needed by unforeseen circumstances;
- in clear demarcation and allocation of activities among a group of people and effectively controlling the course of actions towards achieving the goals;
- in drafting a financially elastic budget for supporting and sustaining the library / information centre; and
- in providing an integrated and yet an analytical projection of the future course of development of the library / information centre.

STEPS INVOLVED IN PLANNING

The following 9 steps can be identified in the planning process:

1. Constituting a Planning Committee;
2. Collecting of all pre-planning data/information;
3. Assessing library needs of the user community;
4. Evaluating current library practices and services
5. Determining the role of the library/information centre
6. Setting goals, objectives, and priorities;
7. Developing and evaluating strategies;
8. Implementing strategies; and
9. Monitoring and evaluating progress.

The whole process can be divided into two phases. Phase 1 will be the Pre-planning phase consisting of steps from 1 to 4, viz. constituting the Planning Committee, collecting all pre-planning information, assessing the library needs, and the evaluation of current library practices and services. Phase 2 of the planning process will include steps from 5 to 9, viz.

determining the role of the library / information centre, setting goals, objectives, and priorities, developing and evaluating strategies, implementing strategies, and monitoring and evaluating progress.

Constitution of the Planning Committee (Step 1)

The Planning committee must be composed of four essential elements, namely representatives of the management, user community, library staff, and at least one library consultant. Much depends upon the personality of the library consultant who must be an experienced library and information science expert. Additional hands to take care of the ICT segment may be provided, if necessary.

Feasibility Study (Steps 2 & 3)

At the pre-planning phase it is desirable that a feasibility study is undertaken with a view to examine the technical viability of the new project. This study should cover three things: the study of the potential clientele, the study of the total information flow in the user community, and the current services and resource of the library / information centre, if applicable. These can be explained one by one.

How to Study the Potential Clientele?

Here our knowledge about the subject User Studies and their techniques will be very helpful. Three types of information, in particular, have to be acquired in this context:

(a) Information on the institutions, projects, and programmes;

(b) Information on particular user groups with their interests and needs; and

(c) Information on individual needs.

(a) Studying Institutional Characteristics: Institutional characteristics have to be studied in order to know the fields of interests of people to be served. Look at the questions that can be asked and the sources of their answers, as given below:

Question (Q) : What are the goals/objectives of the organization / mission / project?

Source (S) : Their internal documents such as the Memorandum of Association, Charter of Incorporation, the Act or Statute by which it is formed, policy speeches and statements, official handbooks, etc.

Q : What are the fields of activity and scope of each discernible activity of the persons involved?

S : Their internal documents, like organizational and functional charts, office manuals showing delegation of powers, duties & responsibilities, etc..

Q : What information do they use or need in order to perform efficiently their respective tasks?

S : The persons concerned: to be gathered through interviews, questionnaires, etc.

Q : Where do they now get the information from?

S : The persons concerned: to be gathered through interviews, questionnaires. etc.

Q : Through what channels and media do they now get the information?

S : Through observation of information flow patterns, study of organizational charts, interviewing and questionnaire based surveys.

Q : Are the information available to them adequate, timely, reliable, and accessible at reasonable cost?

S : To be obtained by surveys through interviews and questionnaires.

Q : Is there among the users an interest in, or awareness of, the value of information and of libraries or an information centres?

S : To be collected through questionnaires, interviews, etc

Q : Can the existing library or information centre be modified for a better information consolidation service or a new information centre needed?

S : Opinions to be collected through surveys and case studies.

(b) Studying User Groups and Their Characteristics : Studying the user groups will involve the need to identify more specifically the potential user groups of the library/ information centre being considered. The focus should be on how diverse are going to be the information requirements of identifiable user groups, in respect of professional objectives, functions, wok patterns, educational backgrounds, language proficiency, demographic and social status data, etc.

(c) Studying Individual Users and Their Characteristics : Also worth knowing are the individual differences in their personal attitudes, educational background, training and experience data, soft skills and competencies, area of specialization and all other details that can affect the types and nature of service to be provided to each. Individual scientists may have their favoured subjects, authors, channels, etc. that may have a direct bearing on user needs.

Studying the Total Information Flow

This has to deal with the information transfer process by which a new idea spreads among members of a social system from its source of creation /invention /generation to its ultimate users. The study of this information transfer process is an essential element in a Feasibility Study for the establishment of the information centre. This is because of two reasons: (1) it throws light on the information transfer process among information users; (2) it also throws light on the information seeking behavior of persons in the concerned disciplines. The study of the total information flow should consist of:

1. Identification of the points of generation and utilization of information;
2. Identification of the sources of information – information transfer media /channels; internal and external resources; formal and informal sources; and documentary and non-documentary sources; and
3. Observation of the information seeking behaviour of information user.

Evaluating Current Library Services and Resources (Step 4)

Several kinds of measures have been suggested in evaluating current library services and resources. They are:

- Efforts = Inputs given
- Performance = Results
- Adequacy of Performance = Satisfaction
- Efficiency = Ratio between efforts and performance
- Process = Reasons for success or failure of programmes.

Library statistics, responses to surveys, performance measures, etc. can contribute to the evaluation of current information centre performance.

Determining the Role of the Library /information Centre (Step 5)

The Planning Committee must have completed the formulation of a Role Statement in relation to:

1. **The purpose of the Library / Information Centre** in relation to the particular mission / project in hand based on the pre-planning information already collected, like:
    - the study of the potential clientele,
    - the study of the total information flow,

- the literature survey of documentary sources;
- survey of institutions around,
- survey of experts in the field, etc.

2. **the collection to be developed;**
3. the information services to be performed;
4. the manpower required; and
5. the Involvement of ICT.

This role statement will vary according to the type of the library / information centre.

Setting Goals, Objectives & Priorities (Step 6)

Goals or targets to be achieved at the end of the planning period have to be definitely identified and stated. The goals will be general and not quantifiable. Also there will be different types of goals, like:

- Service goals including types and levels of services to be provided and the individuals to be serviced;
- Resource management goals. Resources have to be employed for meeting the service goals like collection, staff and facilities;
- Administrative and directional goals – like the development and co-ordination of different divisions, co-operative activities, etc.

Objectives, unlike the goals, are specific and quantifiable: For example are the outcome desired (like increasing the number of persons served by a 25%;) and the measurement of achievements (like 50% of the potential users to be converted to actual users).

Priorities : Very often budget constraints will be there. Hence, after determining the relative importance of different goals and objectives, they have to be ranked in the order of priorities.

OTHER STEPS

(a) Developing and Evaluating Strategies (Step 7)

Strategies are actions to be taken to achieve the goals and objectives. Different strategies may be possible and relevant. But they have to be compared for their cost-effectiveness. Different courses of action will be there but one only has to be chosen.

(b) Implementing Strategies (Step 8)

This has to be cautiously done after taking trial runs under careful observation.

Monitoring and Evaluating Progress (Step 9)

Planning is a continuous process, hence monitoring and evaluating the progress towards active achievement of goals becomes necessary. Such monitoring can lead to reviewing and updating of goals / objective / priorities and to developing of new strategies. Planning is an endless activity; the cycle repeats endlessly.

TOOLS FOR PLANNING

Planning involves estimation and forecasting of the requirements of the different units of a Library or Information Centre. Various tools can be employed in this process of estimation and forecasting. Some of the tools are standardization, work study, time study, system analysis, etc.

INTEGRATED LIBRARY & INFORMATION SYSTEMS

The term Integrated Library & Information Systems (ILIS) is used to mean systems that are designed and implemented for automating every thing that a library needs in its functions and services; these systems are duly coordinated and blended together into a functioning whole. This is unlike and against the earlier systems we were more often familiar with, which were designed for application in specific operations or functions in libraries. Until 1990s library system technologies were confined to computerizing mainly the traditional library functions and operations, like the circulation control, cataloguing, serials control, acquisition work, maintenance of the public catalogue, etc, These systems were fundamentally local with emphasis on controlling and accessing resources within a specific library or even a defined network of libraries. They were not aimed at accessing remote databases or library catalogues. These systems were text-based with no graphics, sound, or multimedia. Their hardware was mainly powerful super computers, minicomputers, or even mainframe computers. But after 1990 there was a speedy transformation in library automation. This was due mainly to the rapid technological changes, which opened up new possibilities in library services and in access to resources even in other locations, It was during this period that Internet opened up, the 'gateways' for individuals to enter the 'cyberspace', and all types of users began to expect their local library to function as the necessary 'launching pad' for them to explore the cyberspace. In the words of John M Cohn, et al (2002) *"the purpose and scope of the library's automated, integrated system was broadened to do more than just computerize manual or paper-based routines. Systems had to connect through the local library or network of libraries, into systems of other vendors, far-flung networks, full-content databases, and, of course, the internet. Accessibility was re-defined to include the ability to obtain resources and information in all formats wherever it was located, from anywhere, at any time, day or night. Thus, 'automating the library' no longer refers only to computerizing operations in a discrete, physical place. it has assumed a wider frame of reference - namely that of enabling the library user to reach beyond what is* ***'merely' local*** *to an information and knowledge base that is truly* ***global and interconnected****",*

STRATEGIC PLANNING (SP)

The main change that has taken place in the recent past

in the concept and process of planning in general has been evident. In the 1960s, long range planning was a logical exercise based on the assumption that present trends would continue into the future and any change would be evolutionary or incremental, In the 1980s, Strategic Planning (SP) emerged as a way of coping with the turbulence, which characterized the contemporary environment, This planning is in effect a process of relating an organization and its products, services and people, to the changing environment and the opportunities and threats in the marketplace. Strategic Planning is a process in which purposes, objectives and action programmes are developed, implemented, monitored, evaluated and reviewed, According to Jo Bryson (1997), SP is "*a disciplined effort to produce, fundamental decisions and actions that shape and guide what an organization, (or other entity) is, what it does and why it does it.*" Strategic Planning is particularly concerned with anticipating and responding to environmental factors, taking responsibility for change, and providing unity and direction to an organization's activities. It differs from traditional long-range planning in its focus on identifying and resolving *issues*, its expectation of new trends and *discontinuities*, and its association with *multiple* futures and *qualitative* shifts in direction. SP has become today the planning method of choice for many organizations in almost every field of endeavour, S P focuses on mainly; two things;

- Identifying key environmental issues influencing the library; and
- Defining a vision of service that describes ultimate outcomes but provides for flexibility in achieving these outcomes,

SP is a relatively new concept in management studies and it is now gaining relevance in library management also. The concept of SP has been already introduced in Chapter 1. There it was mentioned that SP is a pre-condition for Strategic Management (SM). This chapter being devoted to Planning of

Library and Information Systems, the topic of SP deserves to be dealt with here in some detail. Already the term SP was defined in Chapter 1. The following three statements will go to supplement the definition:

1. SP is a process of relating an organization and its products, services and people to the changing environment and the opportunities and threats in the market place.
2. SP is a process in which purposes, objectives and action programmes are developed, implemented, monitored, evaluated and reviewed.
3. SP is a "disciplined effort to produce, fundamental decisions and actions that shape and guide what an organization (or other entity) is, what it does, and why it does it".

According to Jo Bryson (1997) SP is a continuous and proactive process. This process recognizes that organizations cannot achieve everything they would like to do. Instead, it allows for the allocation of resources and planning of strategies on a priority basis to best achieve the organizations' mission within the resource constraints and dynamics of the external environment. The product of this process is called the 'Strategic Plan', which is the written record of the organization's vision, mission statement, its objectives and the mechanisms to achieve them.

Environment & Environmental Scanning

Since SP has to do with essentially environmental factors it is necessary to discuss environmental factors affecting the library and information systems and services. Library and information services do not exist in isolation, They are part of the large environment, but usually exist within a specific organizational context to serve a particular community. Although it is difficult to define the term "Environment" in precise terms, it can be understood as comprising facts and issues that might have a large impact on an organization's performance, but over which it may have little influence although in turn that organization's actions may affect other organizations and individuals. Environment is a complex set of variables for focusing our appraisal and assessment. The process of looking at or looking for information related to the environment is known as **Environmental Scanning.**

The total environment can be broken down into two components, viz: the Macro-environment and the Micro-environment. The Macro-environment may sometimes be referred to as the societal environment; representing the outside world in general or those conditions that have a broad and therefore indirect impact upon the organization. In contrast, factors and forces in the micro-environment have a major and direct effect on the organization and its services. The total environment can be illustrated as follows:

- Macro-environment, i.e. the outside world in general or the external environment.
- Micro-environment or the internal environment. This has to be viewed under three levels:
  - The Task environment, i.e. the sector in which the organization operates;
  - The Corporate environment, i.e. that which covers the organization, its structure, culture, resources, etc.
  - The Stakeholder environment, i.e. the needs and expectations of the stakeholders.

Macro-Environment Analysis

The conventional way of viewing the macro-environment, is to consider issues and influences under four headings: Political, Economic, Social, and Technological **(PEST or STEP) Analysis,** depending on the order in which the headings are listed, There is another formula now in use in environmental scanning, known as the SEPTEMBER Formula, wherein each letter stands for a set of variables. After having known what are the environments to be scanned and analyzed what all are needed to be known now is the methodology for doing the scanning.

In the **SEPTEMBER Analysis Model,** the acronym is formed as follows:

S = SOCIETY

E = ECONOMICS

P = POLITICS

T = TECHNOLOGY

E = EDUCATION

M = MARKETPLACE

B = BUSINESS

E = ETHICS

R = REGULATIONS

Each of the parameters in the formula can be explained as follows:

Society : includes socio-cultural issues and population trends. In the university / college library context it can include the size, nature and content of the user community, like the number of teachers, researchers, PG and under-graduate students, number and variety of teaching and research; departments and other institutions, open university / distance learning facilities, continuing education programmes; non-teaching community and its size, content and nature, management and authorities of the college / university, like the Syndicate, Senate, Academic Council, Boards of Studies, other committees and councils, etc.

Economics : Includes all general specific economic issues and conditions, In the case of the college / university libraries the economic status and stability of the parent institution, the resources at command, the fee structure, government / UGC grants and aids receivable, the possibility of external aids / from funding agencies, self-financing programmes available support of parent-teacher organizations, the paying capacity of parents and students, participation and involvement of the alumni, college owner communities / organizations, etc,

Politics : Includes factors like governrnent stability; public expenditure; industrial policy like privatization, deregulation, etc. In the case of academic libraries the educational policies and programmes of the State and Union Governments, of the ruling parties and opposition parties, the possibility of allocations in the government budgets and Plans, the policy regarding external aid and dependence on government organizations and funding agencies, privatization of education, liberalization and deregulation in running educational institutions etc.

Technology : In the context of library automation, technology involved has components like hardware, software, and human ware, besides communication facilities and connectivity infrastructure, and their state-of-the-art and availability through local vendors / suppliers and their warrantee for updating and maintenance services,

Education : In the context of LIS education includes the levels of education of its user groups, their areas of study, research or specialization, the degree of library and information support needed for each category of users, their interests in general education and knowledge, exposure and experience in computer-based information search, interests in continuing education, skill and competency development of the working folk, their interests in publishing activity, etc,

Marketplace : Includes the nature and range of products, services, customers, partners, suppliers, competitors, etc, in the marketplace, and pertinent factors like growth, maturity and pricing of products and services. In the context LIS, the number of different libraries and information centres functioning in a given area / region / subject / service specialty, the nature and type of their services, the rates of membership subscription taken by other libraries and services, the price / charge levied for various fee-based services, or for access of users to national / international services by the service providers, etc

Business : Includes the general trends and specific developments in the relevant sectors of information industry and business, like price range of books and other publications, data bases of online service providers, the conversion rates of foreign currencies, etc.

Ethics : Value systems, codes of conduct, professional ethics, etc. existing and enforced in the library workplace, the library & information policy of the Government, and the University / College, ethics of the library profession, fee-based services and the rationale behind pricing for specialized services, and the costs reckoned in such pricing, criteria for free or subsidized services in academic libraries, etc.

Regulations : Include every law or regulation or government order, either directly or indirectly related to organizing and functioning information services generally or any type of specialized services in particular. Laws relating to copyrights, patents and other intellectual property rights, data security and privacy, trends in service contracts and licensing agreements prevailing in online services, software trade, etc. may have due relevance in the environment scanned.

Understanding the external environment in which the library or information centre has to operate is fundamental to positioning its services, for adopting new technologies and for obtaining the necessary resources. The external environment is dynamic and needs to be constantly scanned to identify new realities, challenges and uncertainties. Therefore, assessment of the external environment is one of the first inputs into the situation audit stage of the strategic planning process. Jo Bryson has listed the 12 environmental domains that may impact a library and its services (through its parent organization) as follows:

- Economic conditions,
- Availability of financial resources,
- Geographical situation,
- Degree of technological integration and innovation,
- Historical development and parentage of the library and its parent organization,
- Customers and markets,
- Demographic patterns,
- Labour market and industrial relations,
- Availability of resources,
- Industry strata,
- Cultural-social conditions, and
- Political climate.

On closer analysis each of the above listed factors will have a direct or indirect influence on the library and its services, although the degree of influence of each factor can vary. When more factors have stronger influences the external environment of the library becomes very complex.

Micro-Environment Analysis

Understanding the internal environment is an equally important task in SP. The success of an organization in a highly competitive atmosphere, is heavily dependent upon its micro-environment, especially the characteristics of the people involved. Their perceptions, feelings of well being towards the organization, needs and expectations, the interaction of people and structures, the behavioural processes such as leadership style, planning, communications, conflict management, decision making processes, problem solving and interpersonal behaviours, etc may influence the internal environment of the library or information centre. The most likely characteristics of successful organizations are its structure, culture, management style, values, communication, use of technology. etc.

Stakeholder Analysis

Organizations and services do not consist of impersonal entities. They consist of people – individuals and groups. The day-to-day operations and long-term development of these organizations and services depend upon how their people interact with each other, and with the outside world. A stakeholder analysis is a convenient way of identifying people whose opinions and activities affect the organization,

According to Jo Bryson, "*a stakeholder analysis is the means for identifying who the organization's internal and external stakeholders are, how they evaluate the organization, how they influence the organization, what the organization needs from them, and how important they are*". But then, who is a stakeholder? - A stakeholder can be defined as any individual or group with an involvement or interest in the organization, actual or potential, in the past, present or future. In that sense, a stakeholder can be any person, group or organization that can place a claim on an organization's resources, attention or output, or is affected by its output. Examples of the stakeholders of a library or information system include not only its clients or customers (as could be subdivided into various categories, like readers, researchers, borrowers, etc.), but also top management in the host organization, information service staff, funding bodies and other regulators, suppliers, partners, competitors, trade unions, professional associations, and the 'local community'. These groups can usefully be divided into internal and external stakeholders, and also into those directly and indirectly affected by the services, These groups are not mutually exclusive, but often overlapping with the same people featuring under several headings,

Developing a Basic Technology Plan

Planning is the process by which we make decisions about what to do and outline how we will do it. In today's library environment, planning is more critical than ever. Information and Communication Technology has expanded rapidly to include a wide array of systems and services that allow a library to manage locally created information and to access information scattered across the globe. Therefore, it is vital to develop a basic technology plan as a first step in identifying which automated systems and services will best meet user needs and fulfill the mission of the library. In the rapidly changing nature of the library technology, a strategic planning approach is particularly useful in developing plans for automation and technology. This approach in developing a basic technology plan involves the following 8 steps:

1. Assessing existing technology and services.
2. Assessing the environment and client needs,
3. Establishing priorities,
4. Developing your mission, goals, and objectives for action,
5. Developing a preliminary budget proposal to implement the Plan,
6. Evaluating your Plan's accomplishments,
7. Redefining your priorities, as necessary, and
8. Updating and revising your Plan.

In the early nineties planning efforts were focused on shifting from manual to automated circulation control, and computerized public catalogue, Some of the very early adopters of automation later moved on to second-generation systems, but more libraries were automating for the first time, than were migrating from one automated system to another. The first system of many libraries were created to access and manage primarily locally held resources. especially print resources. But, today libraries must be able to access a wide array of resources and databases, in all formats and available anywhere. Users expect seamless access across system platforms to wherever such resources are located. Accordingly, hardware and software products have changed drastically in the last few years. In terms of overall functionality, libraries expect systems that offer:

Comprehensive connectivity to all kinds of systems, including older, 'legacy' systems;

The ability to establish and control external links to remote resources;

The ability to customize the system locally;

Seamless movement between and among functions within the system,

Search engine power and flexibility;

Support for all recognized standards;

Compatibility with the World Wide Web

Whether it is in the case of the first-time system selection or in the subsequent system migration what is crucially important is the planning.

User Expectations

As librarians who are being exposed to current professional literature we know that the user needs vary very much along with the changing information environment. Therefore, there is increased need for careful planning with stakeholder involvement in planning process. We can discern now some overall trends that are characteristic of the expectations of library clientele today. They are listed hereunder (john M. Cohn, 2002):

- Users expect their online library catalogues to perform in the same way as the browsers in the World Wide Web do.

- Users expect not only a seamless integration of resources, but a common, graphical interface through which they can access their resources.
- Users expect quick, if not instantaneous, response time to complex queries across a myriad of databases,
- Users expect all varieties of format of information to be available to them.
- Users want to be able to access the same resources they can get in the library from remote locations such as their homes and offices.
- Users expect to be able to access the library's resources 24 hours a day, 7 days a week.
- Users may expect electronic assistance or mediation to replace or supplement human interaction.
- Users prefer systems that allow maximum opportunity for [1]self-service' features and user-initiated manipulation of system. For example, the ability;
  - to place an inter-library loan request,
  - to reserve a book,
  - to create a list of materials in different formats, or
  - to interactively exchange information with library staff or other users of the library system.

Users want personalization and customization of services, including personal profiles and preferences, topical alerts, and the ability to save fast the research results for on-going reference.

In view of these expanding horizon of user expectations the Basic Technology Plan for an Integrated Library and Information System must be able to co-ordinate and meet successfully each and every one of the user needs.

Cost Estimation

Finally, there is one last point and it relates to the cost involved in the Technology Plan for an Integrated Library & Information System. The Technology Plan should include also a proposed budget, which will form the basis for the preparation of the Annual Budget. There are 10 major cost elements involved in the budget for library automation.

1. Planning and consulting costs.
2. Purchase of system hardware and software.
3. Purchase of network-specific hardware, software, and cabling.
4. Telecommunication and connectivity charges.
5. Conversion of manual records into machine readable form or processing of existing electronic data for use in the new system.
6. Access, and subscriptions where appropriate, to external database and systems.
7. Internet access.
8. Ongoing operating costs.
9. Additions to the system hardware and software.
10. Initial and ongoing training for system operators and library staff.

REFERENCES

BRYSON, Jo.(1997), *Managing information services; an integrated approach,* Hampshire, Gower, 1997.

COHN, John M, et al. (2002), *Planning for Integrated Systems and Technologies; a how-to-do-it Manual for Librarians,* Revised by David Salter, London Facet Publishing,

CORRAL, Sheilla (2000). *Strategic management of information services; a planning handbook,* Taylor & Francis, 2000.

DESS, Gregory B., et al. (2005), *Strategic management, edn.2,* New York, McGraw-Hill Irwin, 2005.

GLUCK, F..W., KAUFMAN, S & WELLECK, A.S.(1982),"The four phases of strategic management", *Journal of Business Strategy*, 2(3); pp.9-21.

MATHEWS, Joseph R. (2005), *Strategic planning and management for library managers*, Greenwood, 2005.

SEETHARAMA, S.(1990), *Guidelines for planning of libraries and information centres*, Calcutta, IASLIC, 1990

WELLS, Denise Lindsey (2015), *Strategic management for senior leaders; a handbook for implementation*, U.S.Dept. of Navy Total Quality Leadership Office, Publication No. 96-03. January1,2015.

WILSON, Alexander (1978). *Planning approach to library management*, London, Library Association, 1978.

5
User Community and Its Requirements

A crucially important step in the pre-planning stage is the collection of data about the User Community and its Requirements. This has been partially covered in the previous chapter where the aspects like assessing library needs of user community and study of the potential clientele were dealt with. In this chapter we will discuss this subject in a larger perspective, namely: Who all constitute the user community of a science library or information system? What are their information requirements? What are the likely sources of the information they need? – both external and internal sources, documentary and non-documentary sources?. Two other topics will also be dealt with in this chapter, namely, 'Customer Relations' and 'Total Quality Management (TQM)'. Both these topics form an integral part of modern management concerned with customer satisfaction and, therefore, are included in this chapter dealing with the management of the User Community of an information system.

USER STUDIES

Normally the users of a science information system, for example the library / information centre of an industrial establishment, can have a wide community of users or stakeholders ranging from policy makers, planners, decision takers, managerial personnel, executives, industrialists, workers, small entrepreneurs, and extension workers, to the rural people who are the ultimate consumers of industrial products and services . The intellectual level of this user community may range from the highly educated to the illiterate.

User Studies has emerged as an important discipline in Library & Information Science today. It had its genesis in the 1930s when Louis R. Wilson (1938) studied the status of libraries in the United Sates. In 1948 and 1958 the Royal Society Scientific Information Conferences were held in London and Washington respectively wherein J.D. Bernal (1948) and Ralph R. Shaw (1956) were the pioneers in User Studies. Bernal studied the use of scientific information based on questionnaire method, whereas Shaw studied the use of scientific literature based on questionnaire and dairy studies, Large amount of user studies came out since then. An important turning point in the history of User Studies was the establishment of CRUS (The Centre for Research on User Studies) by the British Library Research & Development Division, at the University of Sheffield in 1975. According to Prof, Herbert Menzel (1964), User Studies fall into three categories: Behavioural Studies, Information Use Studies, and Information Flow Studies. Behavioural Studies are those that deal with the pattern of overall interaction of the users community with the communication system without reference to any specific information receiving event. Information Use Studies are those conducted to find out the use of any communication medium such as primary journals, secondary journals etc.. Information Flow Studies are those that are conducted to find out the pattern of flow of information in the communication system..

Need for User Studies

User Studies are intended as the systematic approach in evaluating and re-organizing library and information services, and have the following objectives:

1. in judging the efficiency of Library and Information System,
2. in identifying the levels and kinds of user needs,
3. in innovating more cost-effective method of library resources,
4. in enhancing the quality of the collection through changing the collection development programmes,
5. in identifying the problems that reduce or prevent the fuller use of the library and its resources and to find appropriate solutions,
6. in identifying the future information needs and demands, and
7. in designing and developing need-based / user-oriented information system.

Who are the Users?

For all practical purposes, Users are those who use the library and its services at least once in a year. They can be divided either by age, by sex, by occupation, or by subject specialization, etc, But generally, Information Users can also be grouped as :

1. Potential Users (those who need),
2. Expected Users (those intending to use),
3. Actual Users (those who used), and
4. Beneficiary Users (those benefitted).

What Can Be Studied In User Studies?

User Studies may have one or more of the following purposes:

- To know about the range of information sources they use;
- To know about the relative usefulness of the different sources;
- To know about the background, motivation, professional orientation, and other individual characteristics of users;
- To know about the social, political, economic and psychological factors affecting the users;
- To know about the consequences of information uses; and
- To know about anything else.

How to Study the Users?

Information use is a behaviour and data are collected on any behaviour

1. either by asking people about it;
2. or by observing their occurrences;
3. or by examining its artifacts (e.g. documents / proofs).

The methodologies now used are diverse and are applicable to the special problem / phenomena studied.

There are Conventional Methods like Questionnaire, Interview, Diary Study and Observation by Self. Questionnaires may be structured or unstructured. Questions are framed to ascertain the user needs, use patterns and use behaviour. These are in the case of structured questionnaire. Unstructured questionnaire are used for interviews, Two types of interviews also are there – Structured and Unstructured. Structured interviews are conducted by using a predesigned questionnaire. It is possible to study the difference between typical and habitual information use. There are concepts like Critical Incident Information Use, and Information Chunk. The information chunk is the smallest quantity of information required to answer a task related question. The Diary Study has been there since 1948 from the time of Bensal, Diary Recordings reflect the typical behaviour of information users. It may lead to information on a series of critical incidents if the diary relates to an ongoing task.

There are a number of Non-Conventional Methods in User Studies. They are the Solution Development Record, Participant Observer Technique, Sociometric Analysis, Psychometric Method, and Cognitive Organization Studies, Further, there are the Citation Analysis, Computer -based Researches, etc. Also various experiments and quasi-experiments can be set up in field settings.

The Solution Development Record was used first by Allen (1965) where he used Diary recordings of scientist's estimate of the likely solutions to the problems they were working on. The Participant Observer Technique was used extensively by F.H. Cushing (1896) in his study of the Zuni people in the later half of the 19th century, .Here the behaviour of each scientist is observed by a participant observer working as an information assistant for each scientist. He will be trained on record keeping, Sociometric Analysis is a well developed research methodology. This is concerned with the study of the influence of interpersonal relations among scientists. Informal and formal communications are covered by this method. Citation Analysis provides evidences of the use of documentary sources of information, This method was developed by Eugene Garfield (1964) who produced the Science Citation Index, This enabled documentary analysis by plotting the networks of papers and reciprocal citations showing connections among documents rather than people. Experiments and Quasi-experiments can be done in various field settings. Beyond passive observation, experiments can be designed where scientists competing to prepare R & D proposals in response to Government contracts giving opportunities for experimenting with actual situations. The Psychometric Method was first used by Larry R,.Price (2016). In the Psychometric Method two important topics in scientific information use are studied: (1) Motivation, and (2) Cognitive Organization. In Motivation studies it is directed to know why information is sought. There are different motives like achievement motive, curiosity motive, self-evaluative motive, affiliation motive, utility motive (cash/reward), and Ego motive. The limitation is that one's own statement of motives is difficult to validate. In the Cognitive Organization it is studied as to how do scientists approach to locate the desired information. The pattern of approach would match with each user's habit of cognitive organization. They will be using many headings to locate the desired information rather than the few prescribed by classification schemes / thesaurus, etc. The study of the pattern will lead to redesigning the system. Pattern of verbal association through computerized content analysis is also possible. Computer-based research provides opportunities in online systems to derive at information seeking behaviour of scientists more accurately, unobtrusively, measurably, and undefiably with tabulated data. It can also provide immediate feedback with exciting potential for psychometric research.

User Categories and their Needs

The following dominant categories in the user community could be specially considered:

Researchers and scientists – those working in the research & development;

Field workers - those engaged in field operations, like engineers and technicians;

Policy makers and planners; and

Communicators and intermediaries.

We may examine each of these groups and the nature of their dominant needs in some detail.

Researchers and scientists need communication of scientific and technological information:

1. for stimulation of thought and action by injection of / interaction with other people's ideas, knowledge, experience and achievements;
2. for current awareness;
3. for avoiding unnecessary waste and duplication in research efforts;
4. for providing introductory and background information for work in unfamiliar fields (= retrospective type information);
5. for providing specific information and data needed for works in hand (= Current information);
6. for providing necessary problem-solving information;
7. for providing specialized information in one's preferential field of research; and
8. for proper choice of research topics and formulation of working hypotheses.

By their types, information that researchers and scientists require can fall into categories, like:

- S & T information - enabling learning, research, technical decisions and actions;
- Experimental information;
- Know-why information (= scientific);
- Know-how information (= technological);
- Know-who information (= personal).

Policy makers and decision takers will need appropriate information support for their respective functions. For them, problem-solving type answers to their specific queries will have to be found. For decision takers, alternative solutions / strategies to one and the same problem may have to be highlighted.

Planning personnel will need planning, operating and control types of information. In an industrial environment they may pertain to:

- Engineering/ design;
- manufacturing / operations;
- marketing;
- finance / administration;
- project planning / control; etc

Communicators / Intermediaries : Extension workers act as intermediaries for establishing liaison with the generators / innovators of an appropriate technology. For example are: the Biogas Technology, the Fuel Efficient Kilns, and the Chimneys technology. Extension workers need detailed information pertaining to:

the technology itself;

the practical methods for spreading that technology;

the socio-cultural characteristics of the region concerned;

the costs and benefits; etc.

Grouping of Information Needs

On the whole, after taking into account the varied requirements of all the categories of users discussed above, the information required may pertain to the following groups:

- Science & Technology Information
- Economical Information;
- Financial Information;
- Legal Information;
- Geographical Information;
- Climatological Information;
- Socio-cultural information; and
- Environmental Information.

All the above given details will serve as a checklist for equipping and preparing the library or information system for services and operations, especially in building up a purposive collection of materials and resources.

CUSTOMER RELATIONS

Good Customer Relations is an ardent desire of the User Community in Libraries and Information centres. 'Customer Relations' is a business management term and it has relevance in Library and Information System management mainly because some practitioners and teachers in LIS are attracted by such modern management concepts and techniques.

A 'customer' is one who buys some goods or services marketed by a seller. An alternative to 'customer' is the term 'consumer'. Since libraries are not generally engaged in any selling activity they were having neither customers nor consumers. Libraries are service institutions engaged in providing facilities for reading and reference within the library or lending materials for reading outside the library. Other activities of Libraries are helping people in their learning or knowledge acquisition through the supply or dissemination of information in the form of various other products and services. The takers of all these different services and facilities are generally referred to as 'readers' or 'library users'. Another term in general use in LIS is 'library clientele'. Nevertheless, to address a library user as 'customer' may sound to be a misnomer. But, in view of the changing trends in library activities and services particularly the increasing emphasis in marketing of information products and services, and fee-based library and information services where some sort of actual selling and buying are involved, perhaps it is appropriate and relevant to address 'customer relations' as a topic in libraries and information systems.

Customer Relations and Library Management

'Customer Relations' is not at all a new concept in LIS. It was right there in its seminal sense from a very early period although the terminology used then was different. Dr. S. R. Ranganathan, the Father of Library Science in India, held the view that '*reader is always the parameter*' in all aspects of librarianship. In the Five Laws of Library Science he evolved, three Laws were emphasizing the reader, like 'Every reader his book', 'Every book its reader' and "Save the time of the reader'. He also developed techniques and procedures to satisfy the requirements of all the Five Laws. Amongst them the concept of 'Reference Service' he developed was indeed directed towards the ideal customer relations in libraries stressing the personal assistance of the library staff in satisfying the individualistic needs of all types of readers.

Customer Relations & Reference Service

Reference Service was defined by Ranganathan as "*assistance rendered by the librarian in establishing the contact between the right reader and the right book at the right time and in the right personal way*" (Ranganathan (1961), According to him reference service is a sublimated salesmanship wherein the librarian speaks about the library's products and services so as to convince a person about the advantages and benefits that person can derive from the product or service so that the person decides to spare his money, time or energy, to acquire that product or service. Reference service as personal assistance to readers has been envisioned in four types according to the four categories of readers who are to be handled in a library. They are Freshmen (newcomers), General readers, Casual enquirers, and Specialists. Freshmen need Initiation of Freshmen, General Readers need General Help, Casual Enquirers need Ready Reference Service, and Specialist Enquirer needs Long Range Reference Service. In all these services the establishment and maintenance of direct personal relations with the individual client is emphasized. In the Initiation of Freshman, where the newcomer is cordially received and escorted by the library staff for a round inside the library explaining everything that would help the newcomer in putting the library to his best use. In Ready Reference Service and Long Range Reference Service there are prescribed procedures, like the reference interview, user interactions, etc. for the exact enunciation of the problem involved in the reader's enquiry. In the General Help to the General Reader, the library staff always will be on floor duty to monitor, overview and assist the reader as and when individual help is needed. The maximum user satisfaction is the ultimate objective of good library service, and Reference Service goes a long way in building and promoting user satisfaction. In the matter of collection building, readers' suggestions are always taken care of. Even in the case of some modern library services like Current Awareness Services and Selective Dissemination of Information, user needs are ascertained in detail through User Surveys and user profiles are built up and kept updated often through user feedbacks, in order that the services are aptly tuned to the individual needs of users.

Customer Relations & New Age Libraries

In the light of the unprecedented developments in Information and Communication Technology, especially the phenomenal growth of the Internet and the Digital Information Resources, generally people apprehend that libraries and librarians will go obsolete in future. But, for libraries to sustain in the New Age they must be able to adapt, evolve and change as customers continue to learn to use new tools and ways to communicate and receive information. Good customer services will enable libraries not only to survive but also to thrive.

Good Customer Relations

Customer Relations, whether in business management or in LIS management, are almost similar. Management trainers used to caution trainees that *"Customer is the one boss you must please. Satisfying the customer is of prime importance"*. Taking this saying seriously company managers with vision develop their mission statement for their employees as follows:

- A customer is the most important person ever in this office ...in person or by mail.
- A customer is not dependent on us...we are dependent on him.
- A customer is not an interruption in our work... he is the purpose of it. We are not doing a favour by serving him ... he is doing us a favour by giving us the opportunity to do so.
- A customer is not someone to argue or match wits with., Nobody ever won an argument with a customer. A customer is always right. It is very important not to disagree with a customer or make him angry.
- A customer is a person who brings us his wants. It is our job to handle these profitably to him and to ourselves.

The McDonald Model

Satisfied customer is the mark of success in business. McDonalds is an American company which runs a chain of restaurants which has made the marketing of a burger a great success story. Their philosophy, as reported in the *USA Today* (1998) is as follows:

"Everyday an average of 38 million people visit its 23,500 restaurants in 109 countries. People do not swarm to MacDonald's outlets solely because they love the hamburger. Some other restaurants make better-tasting hamburgers. People are flocking to a system not a hamburger. Throughout the world, this fine-tuned system delivers a high standard of what McDonald's calls QSCV - quality, service, cleanliness, and value. McDonald's is effective to the extent that it works with its supplier, franchise owner, employees, and others to deliver exceptionally high value to its customers". In other words, the customers do not hang around McDonalds's due to any kind of addiction to their burgers but to a promise of a value satisfaction. (Sachdeva, 2009).

Customer Relations Programme

Listening to the customers is an important part of the customer relations programme. Like any good management system it is advisable that before someone takes upon oneself the task of running a customer service and satisfaction programme, certain objectives to such a programme should clearly be stated. Some of the elements which most of the customer relations programmes can stipulate can be: Customer philosophy statement; Customer's opinion feedback; Monitoring of customer complaints; Customer suggestion system; Customer education programme, etc.

Communicating with Customers

Communication with customers or to keep in touch with them is the magic that can continue to make customers happy and satisfied. Although different media vehicles can be used here, like verbal communication, audiovisual communication, print materials, advertisements, publicity, special events, websites, e-mails, mobile messages, etc., the spoken word or oral communication is one of the most powerful media that people working in organizations use to accomplish their customer relations goals. The IBM advertising slogan is significant to note: *"Talking creates customers, actions retain customers"*. Oral communications can necessarily be followed by appropriate action programmes.

Some Keys to Good Customer Relations

The following are some of the keys to providing good customer service in a Library:

Courtesy : Be courteous to the customers. Treat them how you like to be treated. By doing so you will bring customers back to your library.

Meeting Customer Expectations : Always try to exceed customers' expectations. Librarian should try not just to meet their expressed needs, but try to help them in a solution oriented basis, perhaps through arranging a document by interlibrary loan, or an article from a database through a document delivery service, etc. Make sure that your customer's requests are fully addressed.

Team Work : Team work and co-ordination are important in customer service. Avoid self-complacence. We must be able to induct colleagues who are perhaps more proficient in an area than we might be. Always direct the customer to the right specialist rather than avoiding the situation. Ideally, customer service should be seamless and efficient giving the user maximum satisfaction with minimal anxiety or stress.

Product Knowledge : Acquire and maintain good product knowledge. The librarian must know the current and anticipated future needs of the customers. As more databases and digital products develop he should know the most valuable of these. He should go to any extent to acquire this knowledge, may be by attending conferences, or by talking with others, or by keeping abreast of literature.

Professionalism : Professionalism is required in all your dealings with the customers. Be confident and take pride in what we know and what we can do to help them so that the customer develops his trust in us..

Some broad principles of good Customer Service in LIS can also be stated hereunder:

- Give the highest priority to personalized customer services.
- Know the likes and dislikes of the Repeat Customers.
- Know the needs of customers so that services can be delivered as expected.
- Own a customer's complaint; follow the proper protocol to fix the complaint and solve the problem. Pacify the customer instantly. Record every instance of customer dissatisfaction.

- Escort guests rather than point out directions.
- Have an immaculate grooming and uniforms.

Customer Relationship Management (CRM)

In business management, CRM is often used as an acronym for Customer Relationship Management which refers to a computerized and software-based approach to handling customer relationships. Often it is considered as part of a holistic management information system (MIS). CRM consists of the processes a company uses to track and organize its contacts with its current and prospective customers. To support these processes, either a special CRM software or a part of the total MIS software, is used, wherein information about customers and customer interactions are entered, stored and accessed by company staff in the different company departments. The overall objective is to improve the services provided to customers, and to use the customer contact information for the targeted marketing. In that perspective. CRM is not that simple as stated above. It is but a combination of policies, processes, and strategies implemented by an organization to unify its customer interaction and provide a means to track customer information. CRM includes many aspects that may relate directly to one another, like Front Office Operations including direct interaction with customers, Face to Face Meetings and discussions, phone calls, e-mails, online services, etc.; Back Office Operations including billing, maintenance, planning, marketing, advertising, finance, manufacturing, etc.; Business relationships including interaction with other companies and partners like suppliers or vendors, retail outlets or distributors, industry networks, like lobbying groups and trade associations; and analysis wherein the above CRM data are analyzed in order to plan target-marketing campaigns, conceive business strategies, and judge the success of CRM activities in terms of market share, number and types of customers, revenue, profitability, etc. Although most people may view CRM as just a software solution the corporate world today is increasingly recognizing CRM as a 'customer centric strategy' for doing business, supported by software.

TOTAL QUALITY MANAGEMENT (TQM)

Quality in service is an important requirement of the user community of a library or information centre which always strive towards achieving maximum customer satisfaction. TQM is an acronym which stands for Total Quality Management. There are other acronyms used to describe same or similar quality management philosophies, like CQI (=Continuous Quality Improvement), TQC (=Total Quality Control), etc. In general, they all provide a framework for implementing effective quality and productivity initiatives that can lead to increased profitability and competitiveness of organizations. TQM particularly is a business management strategy aimed at embedding quality consciousness in all organizational processes. As a modern management tool TQM has been widely used in all types of organizations and not only in manufacturing industries. Libraries and Information Systems, being a special category of service industry, have a great potential for effective application of TQM because complete customer satisfaction through quality in products and services is their avowed objective.

Objectives of TQM

The following definition will explain what are the principal objectives of TQM.

"TQM is a management approach for an organization, centered on quality, based on the participation of all its members and aiming at long-term success through customer satisfaction, and benefits to all members of the organization and to society" (ISO 8402:1994).

We may analyze this definition to know the main attributes of TQM, as follows:

- a management strategy
  - which is for long term success,
  - which is quality-centered,
  - which is implemented through full participation of all members,
  - which is aimed at customer satisfaction, and
  - which is aimed at benefits to all members of the organization and to society.

Evidently, quality improvement towards maximum customer satisfaction and thereby greater benefits to all members of an organization and to the society as a whole are the principal objectives of TQM.

Origin and Development of TQM

The ideation of TQM philosophy is generally attributed to Dr. W. Edwards Deming, who devised in the 1030s a statistically controlled management process and who could profitably experiment it in the war production plants. Thereupon, the U.S. Department sent him to Japan in 1947 with a mission to revitalize the war-devastated Japanese economy. Deming introduced his statistical process control (or statistical quality control) programmes into Japan's then ailing manufacturing sector which could instill a new dedication to quality and productivity in the Japanese industrial and service sectors and that enabled the country to become a dominant force in the global economy by 1980s. This made U.S. producers also to adopt the techniques of Deming to restore their lost competitiveness. The "Deming Management Method" became the model for many American corporations under the phrase "Total Quality Management", by the late 1980s. Through this the U.S. manufacturing sector had achieved marked gains in quality and productivity by the 1990s. Many major companies have implemented TQM, including Ford Motor Company, Phillips Semiconductor, SGL Carbon, Motorola and Toyota Motor Company.

TQM Compared to ISO 9001

The concepts and principles of TQM have crept into the evolution of the ISO 9001 Management Quality System standard, and later for the ISO 9001:2000 standard's "Process Model". If ISO 9000 is a Quality System Management Standard, TQM is a philosophy of perpetual improvement. The ISO Quality Standard sets in place a system to deploy policy with verifiable objectives. An ISO implementation is a basis for a Total Quality Management implementation. Where there is an ISO system, about 75 percent of the steps are common to TQM. Therefore, the requirements of TQM can be considered 'ISO Plus'. The proposed changes in ISO Standard for its next revision will include Customer Satisfaction and Measurement. In short, implementing TQM will correspond to implementing ISO Standard also.

The three Elements of TQM

TQM is the concept that 'quality' can be managed and that the 'quality management' is a process. The three elements in the TQM process are: "Total", "Quality" and "Management".

Total = Quality involves everyone and all activities in the company.

Quality = Quality is in conformance to requirements (Meeting Customer Requirements).

Management = Quality can and must be managed.

TQM is a process for managing quality; it must be a continuous way of life; a philosophy of perpetual improvement in everything we do. What then is quality? *"Quality is fitness for purpose"* (Juran, 1967) *"Quality is meeting the requirements of customer - now and in the future" (Robinson, 1996). "Quality of a product or service is the ability of the product or service to meet the customer's requirements"* (Sarkar, 1998). These quoted statements (Thakuria, 2007) make the quality concept almost clear to everyone. Quality is thus something concomitant with customer satisfaction.

Improving Quality by Improving Processes

Business managers believe that the key to improving quality is to improve the processes that define, produce and support our products. Therefore, processes must be managed and improved. This involves the following 8 steps:

- Defining the process.
- Measuring the process performance.
- Reviewing the process performance.
- Identifying the process shortcomings.
- Analyzing the process problems.
- Making a change in the process.
- Measuring the effects of the process change.
- Communicating the process change to both the providers and the users.

Principles of TQM

The proponents of TQM have the following basic assumptions or principles, that

- Quality can and must be managed;
- Every employee is responsible for quality;
- Processes, not people, are the problem;
- Problems must be prevented, not just fixed;
- Quality improvements must be continuous;
- Plan and organize for quality improvement; and
- Goals are to be based on requirements, not negotiated.

For any TQM programme in order to be successful the following are essential pre-conditions:

- Knowing the customers.
- Setting the goals based on true Customer Requirements.
- Pursuing a Continuous Improvement Strategy.

- Using a structured methodology for Process Improvement.

TQM in Libraries and Information Systems

The earlier sections were dealing with TQM as it was developed and is being practiced in companies or business establishments. Nevertheless, TQM has a great potential for application in Libraries and Information systems management. In fact, TQM existed in the LIS sector ever since the evolution of the subject although the terminology varied. Earlier efforts at quality management manifested as various assessment methods like User studies, Cost-benefit analysis, Cost-effective studies, Performance Evaluation based on Performance Indicators, Evaluation of Information Storage and Retrieval Systems based on Recall and Precision ratio, etc. In the later years, Quality Assurance studies based on ISO:9000 and other accreditation schemes were conducted in countries like UK, USA and Canada in special libraries and academic libraries. The Harvard College Library implemented TQM in 1993. But in Indian libraries TQM was late to emerge, although more and more research studies in this line are being reported now.

Good management requires that the library maintains Total Quality standard in all aspects of its products and services. But quality is both a user-oriented and a production oriented expression (Bindhu P. Nair, 2008). From the user's point of view, quality is an expression of the usefulness of the products/services in meeting the needs and expectations, in terms of their accuracy, reliability, completeness, timeliness, relevance and so on. From the production point of view, the quality of a product is determined by the quality of its performance which depends on the quality of its design and the quality of its conformance to customer requirements and standards. According to Joseph Jablonski (1992) the three characteristics necessary for TQM to succeed within any organization are: Participative Management, Continuous Process Improvement, and the Utilization of Teams. These we can examine in the case of a library.

Participative Management, refers to the intimate involvement of all library staff in the quality management process, thus de-emphasizing traditional top-down management methods. In other words, senior professionals should set policies and make key decisions, only with the input and guidance of the subordinates who are to implement and adhere to the directives. This technique improves upper management's grasp of operations and, more importantly, is an important motivator for library staff who begin to feel like they have control and ownership of the process in which they participate.

Continuous Process Improvement, the second characteristic, entails the recognition of even small, incremental gains toward the goal of total quality. Large gains are accomplished by small, sustainable improvements over a long term. This concept necessitates a long-term approach by managers and the willingness to invest at present for benefits that may manifest themselves in the future. Speaking in the context of a library or information system, no product or service should be allowed to remain stagnant for long. There is always scope for improvement in the products and processes in the library's march towards Total Quality. In the context of our present day emphasis on information marketing and fee-based services in libraries, every improvisation or improvement in available products or services will have its due returns on investments.

Team work, the third necessary ingredient for the success of TQM, involves the organization of cross-functional teams within the library. This multi-disciplinary team approach will help library staff to share knowledge, identify problems and opportunities, and derive at a comprehensive understanding of the tasks involved in the over-all process of TQM.

Customer Satisfaction in Libraries

In an earlier section we have seen that quality in service is something concomitant with customer satisfaction. This means that if one is there the other is also there. In the library context this statement is directly emphasizing user satisfaction. There are different types and categories of library users. Their requirements are often individualistic. How do we try to ensure the maximum user satisfaction? User satisfaction is largely based on the following:

(a) Quality of information served, decided by its correctness, completeness, timeliness, usability, and speed of service delivery etc. This is the main factor governing user satisfaction. Nevertheless, there are also several others that go to decide the user's overall impression about the library, like:

(b) Physical location and accessibility to the library and its services.

(c) Usefulness of the collection, its nature, coverage, size, and up-to-datedness, its technical organization, shelf arrangement and display,

(d) Physical facilities in the library, like space, furniture, the welcoming internal atmosphere, cleanliness, comfort, etc.

(e) Quality of staff, their courtesy & welcoming attitude, friendliness, communication, professionalism, readiness for help, trustworthiness, etc.

Quality improvement, therefore, has to concentrate on improving the User Satisfaction rating which ought to be continuous improvement programme of the library. Perhaps, one major task involved will be matters relating Human Resources Development oriented to maximum user satisfaction objective.

Quality Measurement in Libraries

Can quality of library and information products or services be measured in quantitative terms? These days we may come across more and more studies in LIS literature about TQM in Indian libraries. They are generally dealing with measuring the quality of available products and services through user studies and assessing customer satisfaction. There are also now in use some important management tools for measuring the quality of library and information products and services, like Performance Measurement (PM), SERVQUAL, LibQUAL, etc. While the first two are developed for business management the last one is specially developed for measuring quality in library and information services. These will be discussed in detail in a subsequent chapter.

CONCLUSION

In the LIS field, the TQM concept was implicitly practiced from very early times even though the same terminology was not used. In fact, topics like User Studies, Cost-benefit Analysis, Cost-effectiveness Studies, Performance Evaluation, Evaluation of Information Retrieval systems using Precision and Recall ratios, etc. had their major focus on the quality of products and services and the degree of user satisfaction obtainable. In LIS 'quality' is often gauged by user-based and value-based approaches. High quality standards meant quality to meet fully the user's requirements and to justify the value paid or investment involved. Quality sometimes was reckoned in terms of the performance of the system as a whole, or the quality and size of the document store, the quality of the information products judged in terms of some defined norms or criteria, user satisfaction in terms of the value of the money spent (cost-benefit) and the value of information content of the product (cost-effectiveness), etc. Therefore, quality management strategies of libraries and information centres were aimed at integrating the various approaches in achieving improved quality of information products and services, like accuracy, adequacy, and timeliness of content. Knowing the user and user requirements is the most important precondition for TQM strategies. "*Quality is what one needs and wants, not what you think is needed or what is convenient for you to deliver*" (Riggs,1992). Quality Assurance studies were at first practiced in special libraries and academic libraries only, based on ISO:9000 and other accreditation schemes, in countries like UK, USA and Canada. But they were late to emerge in Indian libraries. There are now some management tools available for the service quality measurements. These are now found increasingly used in library studies and research. We will find these described in the chapter on Evaluation..

REFERENCES

BARNARD, Susan B, (1997)'Total Quality Management' in *Encyclopaedia of Library and Information Science*, (Ed by Allen Kent & Harold Lancour) Vol. 61 (1997): pp. 311-25., Marcel Dekker.

BAVAKUTTY, M. and ABDUL MAJEED , K.C.(2005), Methods for measuring quality of libraries. New Delhi, Ess Ess Publications, 2005.

BERNAL,J.D. et al (1948) "The Royal Society Scientific Information Conference" *Nature* 162;279-286, (1948).

BINDHU P. NAIR(2008), 'User's perspective on Total Quality Management in Kerala University Library: an analytical study', *KELPRO Bulletin* 12(2), Dec. 2008, Pp.74-94.

CUSHING, Frank Hamilton (1896) Zuni Folk Tales, Good Press publishers, 1896

DEMING, W. Edwards (1982),. *Out of the Crisis*, MIT Centre for Advanced Engineering Study,1982.

DEMING, W. Edwards (1986) *Out of the Crisis: Quality, Productivity and Competitive Position*, Cambridge university Press,1986.

DEMING, W. Edwards,(1993) *The New Economics for Industry, Government and Education*, Boston, Ma, MIT Press,1993

GARFIELD, Eugene (1964), The Sciene Citation Index, Clarivate Analytics

GARFIELD, Eugene (1955) "Citation Indexes for Science; A New Dimension in Documentation through Association of Ideas", *Science* 122 (3159), PP.108-11.

HIAM, Alexander (1992),. *Closing the Quality Gap; Lessons from America's*

Leading Companies, Prentice Hall, Inc. 1992.

JABLONSKI, Joseph R.(1992), *Implementing TQM Competing in the Nineties Through Total Quality Management* Edn. 2. Technical Management Consortium, Inc. 1992.pp.64—76.

JURAN, Joseph M. (1974), *Quality Control Handbook*, New York, MacGraw-Hill.

MENZEL, Herbert (1964) "The Information Needs of Current Scientific Research" *The Library Quarterly; Information, Community, Policy*, Vol.34 (1), Jan 1964 pp 4-19.

PRICE, Larry R, (2016), *Psychometric Methods: Theory into Practice*, The Guilford Press, New York, 2017.

RANGANATHAN, S.R. (1957), *Five Laws of Library Science*, Edn. 2 Bombay, Asia Publishing House, 1957.

RANGANATHAN, S.R.(1961), *Reference Service*, Edn.2, Bombay, Asia Publishing House, 1961.

RIGGS,(1992), "TQM quality improvement in new clothes", *College & Research Libraries* 53(6), 1992 pp.481-482

ROBERTS, Harry V. and Bernard F, Sergesketter (1993), *Quality is Personal: A Foundation for Total Quality Management*. The Free Press, 1993.

ROBIINSON, Bruce Murray (1996), *Total Quality Management in Education: the empowerment of a school community*, Lincoln, University of Nebraska.

SACHDEVA, Iqbal S. (2009), *Public relations; principles and practices*, New Delhi, Oxford University Press, 2009.

SARKAR, D. (1998), *The Manager's Handbook for Total Quality Management*, Beacon Books, 1998.

SHAW, Ralph R. (1956), *Pilot Study on the Use of Scientific Literature by Scientists*, Department of Agriculture, National Science Foundation, U.S.

THAKURIA, Pranjit Kumar ((2007),.'Concept of Quality in Library Services; an overview' in *5th Convention Planner 2007* Guahati University, Dec.7-8, 2007. Pp. 412-

VERMA. R.K.(2002), 'Measuring quality management level with reference to ISO 9000 and TQM for Special Libraries in India', *Annals of Library & Information Studies*, 49(4), 2002 Pp.141-63.

WILSON-DAVIS, K. (1976) "CRUS-its Functions and Aims", *Library Review*, 1 May 1976

WILSON, Louis R. (1938).The Geography of Reading; a study of the distribution and status of libraries in the United States, Chicago, University of Chicago Press, 1938.

6
Collection Devlopment and Management

After having covered the study of the User Community and its requirements now we pass on to the important activity of planning and development of a collection so as to form the basis of a Science Information System. Collection Development is *"a term which encompasses a number of activities related to the development of the library collection, including the determination and coordination of selection policy, assessment of needs of users and potential users, collection use studies, collection evaluation, identification of collection needs, selection of materials, planning of resource sharing, collection maintenance and weeding"* (ALA 1996, p.45). These activities can be broadly grouped into three areas: Study of the Information Sources, Study of the collection building activities, and Study of the Technical Organization of the collection. These aspects are discussed in detail in this chapter.

INFORMATION SOURCES

Generally, two categories of information sources have to be visualized: **Documentary sources**, and **Non-documentary sources**. The first category can be further sub grouped into Printed, Non-printed, and Processed documents. There can be different species of printed documents, like books, journals, reports, patents, standards, etc. Similarly in the class of Non-printed sources there can be different species, like Archives, Manuscripts, and Graphic productions. In the category of Processed documents occur Microforms, like microfilms, microfiche, etc. and the Audio/Video documents. In the modern context, there is a very significant category called the 'electronic resources', consisting of e-journals, e-books, and other databases, whether they are accessible as online, or as offline sources like CDs and DVDs. All documentary sources of information can be further classified into Primary, Secondary and Tertiary documents. The following table gives an overall view of the information sources:

(A) DOCUMENTARY SOURCES:

- **Printed sources**
  - Books
  - Monographs
  - Periodicals
  - Technical Reports
  - Patents
  - Standards
  - Conference proceedings
  - Pamphlets, Leaflets, Brochures, etc.
- **Non-printed sources**
  - Archives
  - Manuscripts
- **Processed documents**
  - Microfilms
  - Audio/Videos
- **Electronic Resources**:
  - Digitized documents
  - e-Journals
  - e-Books
  - Websites
  - Blogs
  - Social media

(A.1) PRIMARY DOCUMENTS:

- Books, Journals, Serials,
- Thesis & Dissertations
- Technical / Research reports,
- Patents & specifications, Standards,
- Data sheets, Drawings, Photographs.
- Charts, Maps and Atlases,
- Drawings, Photographs, Charts.
- Trade Catalogues,
- Lecture notes, Files of correspondence, Memoranda, etc.

(A.2) SECONDARY DOCUMENTS:

- Indexing journals / services
- Abstracting journals / services
- Various types of Current Awareness bulletins/ services
- Ad hoc bibliographies, Documentation lists,
- Various Bibliographical sources and Trade Catalogues, etc..

(A.3) TERTIARY DOCUMENTS:

- State of the art reports
- Trend Reports
- Reviews and digests (like Annual Review series /Progress in series)
- Survey series/Year's Work series
- Information locating tools such as Directories, Glossaries, Handbooks
- and Guide books, Statistical tables, Manuals, etc.

(B) NON-DOCUMENTARY SOURCES:

(B.1) PERSONAL SOURCES:

- Colleagues in the organization
- Peers outside the organization (within the country & outside)
- Information Gate Keepers
- Guides, Advisors, Consultants
- Vendors, Contractors, Collaborators, Licensors, etc.

(A directory of these personal sources should be compiled and maintained).

(B.2) INSTITUTIONAL SOURCES:

- Partner institutions
- Institutions in same and related fields
- Libraries & Information Systems
- Libraries
- Documentation Centres
- Information Analysis Centres,
- Referral Centres, etc.
- Online Networks
- Local Databases
- CD-ROMS/DVDs

Fig. 6.1. Table Showing Variety Of Information Sources

A wide variety of information sources has now come to know about from the Table given above. This table can be used as a Check List for either surveying and auditing the existing collection, or identifying gaps and those that are to be acquired and added to the collection.

Primary Sources of Information

These are the first published records of original research and development or description of new application or new interpretation of an old theme or idea. These are original documents representing unfiltered original ideas and therefore they constitute the latest available information. A researcher producing new information can disseminate the same and make it available to the user community through primary sources. Often it may be the only source of information in existence. Primary sources are often unorganized and are rather difficult to identify and use. A subject becomes a discipline in its own right when independent primary sources begin to be produced in that area. The rate of growth of a discipline to a large extent depends upon the amount of literature being produced in the form of primary sources reporting development in the concerned field.

Secondary Sources of Information

While primary sources are often unorganized and difficult to identify and locate the secondary sources help in both their identification and use. Secondary sources are those which are either compiled from or refer to primary sources of information. The original information having been casually modified selected or reorganized so as to serve a definite purpose for groups of users. They contain organized repackaged knowledge rather than new knowledge. Due to their very nature, secondary sources are more easily and widely available than primary sources. These not only provide digested information but also serve as bibliographical key to primary sources of information. It is convenient to divide the secondary sources into three types which are as follows: 1. Index Type: which contain indexes, bibliographies, indexing periodicals, and abstracting periodicals; 2. Survey Type which includes, reviews, treatises, monographs, and 3 Reference Type: including encyclopedias, dictionaries, handbooks, manuals, and critical tables (Bonne, George S.,1971).

Tertiary Sources of Information

People can rarely differentiate between secondary and tertiary sources. These are materials in which the information from secondary sources are either digested, reformatted or condensed and put it into a convenient, easy to read form. Tertiary sources of information contain generally information distilled and collected from primary and secondary sources. The primary function of such tertiary sources is to aid the information searcher in the use of primary and secondary sources of information. Due to the increase in literature, tertiary sources are becoming increasingly important. Tertiary sources include the following types: Bibliography of bibliographies, Directories and Yearbooks, Guides to literature, Lists of research in progress, etc.

Non-documentary Sources

Non-documentary sources of information form a substantial part of communication especially in science and technology, User's studies have underlined the importance of such sources. These sources provide information which other sources do not, The following types of the sources are worth considering: Formal sources, like those emanate from Research organizations, Societies, Industries, Government departments, Universities, and Consultants. Informal sources like conversation with colleagues, visitors, attendance at professional meetings, etc.

Specific Types of Information Sources

Some popular types of information sources are described below:

Periodicals : All periodicals are not primary sources. But there are many a periodicals which publish first time original works and therefore fall in the category of primary documents. There are many periodicals which specialize in interpreting and giving opinions on developments reported in primary sources of information. Such periodicals may be considered secondary sources.

Indexes : An index to a work contains an alphabetical list of names, topics, places, formulae, titles of any significant item referring to material presented in the main part of the work. Sometimes, these items may be arranged chronologically, geographically or in some other way. A well compiled index adds to usefulness of a work.

Indexing Periodicals : An indexing periodical is a regularly issued compilation of titles of articles that appear in current primary source journals. Generally, titles of new books, pamphlets, etc, are also included.

Abstracting Periodicals : An abstracting periodical "*is a regularly issued compilation of concise summaries of (i) significant* *articles (often in a very limited subject field) that appear in current primary source journals and (ii) important new research monographs, reports, patents, and to the primary source publication in that field"* (Bonne, George S, 1971). An abstracting periodical serves as an index, a tool for retrieval of information on a specific subject. However, indexing periodicals are earlier to appear than abstracting periodicals.

Reviews (Survey Type) : A review is a survey of the primary literature in the concerned subject field. It aims to digest and correlate the literature over a given period. It also indicates the development and trends in the field concerned, such as trend reports and progress reports. It may appear as a collection of papers on regular basis (annual or quarterly or monthly) or in the form of an article in a periodical. A review provides background information to a new problem in a suitable form and serves as a key to literature. List of references given in a review can serve as an excellent bibliography of the concerned subject for a period covered by it.

Reference Books (also considered tertiary) : Reference works, which contain the desired information itself, are considered secondary sources of information. The important types of ready reference books are: Dictionaries, Encyclopedias (also considered tertiary), Handbooks, Tables, Manuals, Textbooks, Translations, Treatises, Monographs, Biographical works, Literary criticisms, etc.

Bibliographies : A bibliography is an organized list of primary or other sources relating to a given subject or person. It is usually arranged alphabetically by author or chronologically or topic wise. It may be comprehensive or selective. Sometimes, it may be provided with annotations. It may be published as a part of a larger work or as a separate work. The basic aim of a bibliography is to assist the users in locating the existence of or identifying a book or any other material which may be of interest to him. A well prepared bibliography provides a definite coverage of documents over a period of time within specified limits. Thus, it also serves the purpose of retrospective searching of literature.

The above categorization is based on the characteristics of the documents. Primary sources are more current and accurate than secondary and tertiary sources. In searching for information, a researcher usually starts with secondary and tertiary sources and ends the search with primary sources. Secondary and tertiary sources contain information in organized form and these serve as guides or indicators to detailed contents of primary literature. With increasing amount of literature being produced, it is becoming almost impossible to use primary sources directly for searching of information. A scholar would also not be able to keep himself up to date and well informed in his field of specialization without the aid of secondary and tertiary sources. This goes to show the importance of the information sources in literature search and research. (Anamika Varshney; *2011).*

COLLECTION BUILDING

Collection development is a challenging activity Collection building is a very crucial part of Library / Information system planning and establishment. After having studied the user community and its character and composition, the information needs of all different classes and types of users, and the information sources available, the next logical step is collection building and the systematic and regular building up of a library's holdings by way of periodical evaluation of the existing collection, the user group analysis, selective acquisition of new items, and even weeding out the unnecessary ones. The basic elements in the collection development process are depicted in the form of an endless cycle (See figure given below).

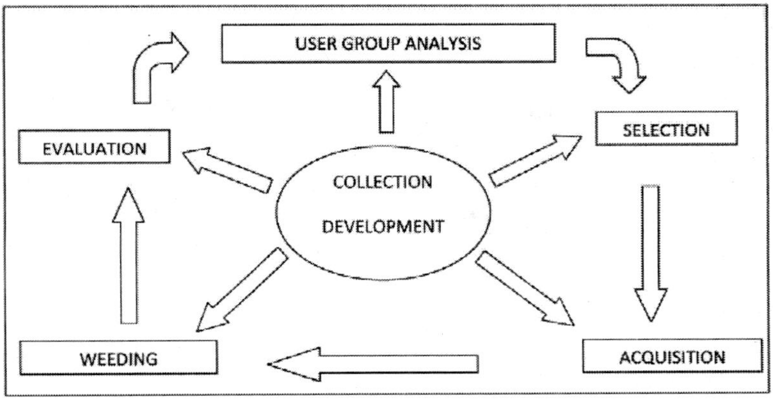

Fig. 6.2. Table Showing Cycle of Collection Development Process
***Source*: Sharma, S. et al *DESIDOC Bull of Inf.Tech.*,1994;14(2) P.1-11**

Guidelines for Collection Building

Collection development is both an art and a science, combining the professional elements of knowledge, experience and intuition. Choices of the collection manager must reflect the needs and interests of community of users (Peggy Johnson ,2004). Collection development involves selection of materials, procurement of the selected items, and taking the procured items into stock. Compared to public and academic libraries, collection development in special libraries is much easier because, special libraries have a generally homogenous user community and a limited subject area of concern. However, some general guidelines for collection building in a science library / information system can be given here:

Collection building should not be arbitrary and haphazard, that is, it should not be without any order or plan of action. On the contrary, It should be based on definite objectives and planned out strategies. It should be based on a **written Collection Development Policy**. The major factors to be considered in collection development are:

1. the programmes of the parent institution to be supported by the library / information system, like its research and development, teaching, general information services, etc.
2. the subject boundaries / coverage of the collection (to be identified based on objectives of the parent body, the user needs, the programmes both at present and in the future).
3. the priorities and limitations governing the collection development, like the degree of continuing support for strong collections / funds; materials already available; physical forms preferred such as books / journals / and other micro-documents, processed and digital information; languages and geographical areas to be covered or excluded; chronological periods to be covered or excluded; duplications and extent of duplication desirable; possibilities of co-operation in collection development / subject specialization; and resource sharing possibilities.
4. The Five Laws of Library Science should be taken as the basic guideline for formulating objectives / policies and procedures of collection development. In this regard, Bhattacharrya of the DRTC, Bangalore, in 1982, had listed some of the basic principles and policies derived from the Five Laws of Library Science. They are stated here:
   (a) Identify the 'Umbral' and 'Penumbral' and 'Alien' areas in the subjects to be represented as is in the APUPA pattern.
   (b) Procure as exhaustively as possible in the Umbral areas, if not easily accessible through Resource Sharing arrangements;
   (c) Depend as much as possible on inter-library co-operation in the Penumbral areas;

(d) Depend entirely on inter-library co-operation in the case of the Alien region;

(e) In procurement of materials prefer the order, namely, 'Gratis- Exchange- Purchase';

(f) If a part of the document (by copying) can serve the need, prefer it to the whole document;

(g) Prefer microform to the macro-form if it serves the purpose;

(h) Follow the principle "The best for the largest at the least cost".

Factors Governing Major Decisions

In collection building and development, the crucial decisions to be taken are based on the questions:

- what to buy?
- what to keep?
- What to borrow?
- What to access off-line?
- What to access on online?

There are also other factors to be considered in making the above decisions:

- The existing collection – its strength and weakness;
- Publishing trends of all types of new materials;
- Estimation of additions needed over a period;
- Estimation of likely fluctuations in budget;
- Identification of priorities – areas /disciplines, documents, etc;
- Availability of shelving space;
- Use made of the existing collection based on library statistics.

Selection of Tools & Aids

What all are the sources of information about individual items belonging to the categories of materials to be considered for selection? Librarians should be able to acquire intimate knowledge about all the various selections tools and aids that are available, not only in the case of books but also for other categories of documents like periodicals, technical reports, patents and specifications, standards, annual reports, audiovisual materials, and every other category of informational material that is going to be covered in the collection building programme. Mention is made below about the major sources of selection tools that can help in respect of some important categories of materials.

Selection of Books

In the case of books, normally, an initial selection is made **firstly**, on the basis of readers' suggestions or intends made by researchers / scientists/ engineers, **secondly** based on book reviews found in either exclusive reviewing journals, or subject periodicals, **thirdly** based on data gathered from the different classes and kinds of bibliographies.

Bibliographical sources are a vast area which includes mainly subject bibliographies, national bibliographies, trade catalogues, bibliographies of reference books, etc. For retrospective and cumulative listing of **currently in-print books**, sources like *Books in Print* and the *Subject Guide to Books in Print* (R R Bowker), *Cumulative Book Index* (H W Wilson), *British Books in Print*, *Whitaker's Cumulative Book List*, the *Indian National Bibliography*, *Indian Books in Print*, etc. are the most consulted traditional book selection tools. The *British National Bibliography*, the *National Union Catalogue of Library of Congress, the Indian National Bibliography, etc.* with their periodical supplements are very dependable sources for books published in the respective countries. Besides all these, the catalogues, flyers and announcements frequently issued by individual publishers or distributors are regularly scanned by librarians. **Current book reviewing sources** are mainly Whitaker's *Book Seller* and *Books of the Month*, R R Bowker's *Publishers Weekly*, and others like *American Book Publishing Record, Book Review Digest* and *Book Review Index* will provide information about current books. In respect of **Reference Books** as a special category, the most outstanding source is perhaps, *the New Walford Guide to Reference Sources* (Facet Publishing, London, 2005) in 3 volumes of which Vol. I is dealing with Science, Technology and Medicine.

While all the above mentioned sources are general in nature and content there are ever so many subject special tools. One must be able to search out the most relevant ones. For example are the *Reference Sources in Science and Technology* by Libraries Unlimited which is a series on different subjects, like the *Guide to Reference and Information Sources in Plant Biology*, or the *Guide to Reference and Information Sources in Zoological Sciences*, etc.

A **fourth** set of book selection sources are the **online databases**, like the online catalogues of major libraries of the world, *the OCLC database*, the *LC-Marc file* and the *Library of Congress Alert Service*, the *RLIN Online*, the *British Library Collections of Scientific Technical and Medical Information, Digital Library of India* of the Indian Institute of Science, Bangaluru, etc. Almost complete catalogue data about the chosen titles can be collected from these sources.

A **fifth** option in book selection is that books found useful can be chosen at book fairs or from among the items supplied by local vendors on 'Books on Approval" basis. The World Book Fair being held in Delhi every year is a great opportunity for librarians and subject experts to see and select books of all types and in all subjects. Also the local book fairs do almost the same service.

A **sixth** option is that libraries can make standing arrangements with important publishers for the supply of all new titles as and when published 'on books on approval basis'.

All items initially chosen, from whatever sources and in whatever manner, are finalized for purchase only after approval by a **Selection Committee** consisting of experts. Some key characteristics considered about books are Author, Publisher, Date of publication, Topic and content, Targeted level of readers, Language, Readability, Physical features of the book like format, binding, illustrations, typography, and finally Price.

Selection of Periodicals

Selection of journals and other serials should be based only on actual or potential need and relevance because of the often prohibitive cost of subscription involved. Then, how to proceed with such a selection process? Perhaps, to start with, **a core collection of journals** has to be ensured. This can be done based on a systematic citation analysis with a view to find out the most relevant journals based on the frequency of citations. This citation study can be done either locally or take help from earlier studies made by others in the subject area concerned. The Institute for Scientific Information (ISI) under Eugene Garfield, has been publishing regularly the *Science Citation Index*. ISI studies have made it possible to spot the most cited journals in particular disciplines. ISI may provide on request ad hoc services like identification and listing of core journals in a suggested discipline, or Impact Studies on specific journals, or authors. The *Ulrich's Periodicals Directory* is a dependable tool for collecting required data about particular journal titles. Before finally deciding to subscribe for any periodical or serial there are some different options to be considered.

Firstly, there may be a possibility of resource sharing arrangements with other physically accessible libraries. It is always more prudent to spend on a new title rather than duplicating the one which is accessible in the neighborhood.

Secondly, the possibility of subscribing to the electronic version, if any, of the required periodical.

Thirdly, the Consortia arrangements that may be available to the library.

In the last two cases there will be considerable cost gains to the library. All these measures can be profitably employed by the Librarian in building up a purposive and cost-effective periodicals collection.

Selection of Technical Reports

Another significant document category for a science library is the Technical Reports. There is no accurate estimate of the number of Reports already available or are being produced every year. It may vary from 1,00,000 to 5,00,000 titles per year. All agree that Technical Reports are an important formal 'primary communication channel' in Science & Technology. About 80 - 85 per cent of the world's report literature is of US origin, and probably over 90 per cent of the US or Foreign origin go through the input of five US agencies, namely, DDC, NASA, DOE, NTIS and ERIC. The bibliographic control and distribution of unclassified technical reports have been so much commercialized by the agencies that it becomes very costly and complex for a library to avail the services of such agencies. "*India too is potentially rich, but lacks a national agency to organize and explore this resource. At present many of the Indian R&D reports can be more easily located and purchased from agencies of information rich countries than within the country. The situation is well exploited and encashed by foreign agencies and their Indian agents*". (Sridhar, M.S. p.78). Librarians have to spare substantial time and efforts to study and understand the complexities involved in locating and procuring technical reports. Many are the usual problems involved like proliferation, lack of bibliographic control, lack of quality control, barriers of security-classification, content duplication possibilities, etc. Added to these, Indian librarians are facing problems in the efficiency and effectiveness of suppliers, problems of economy, problems related to physical conditions of the report documents, etc. NTIS is the biggest self-sustaining commercial source for Reports. Announcement bulletins, like *GRA&I* of the NTIS, *STAR* of NASA, Catalog of ESA, etc, are the vehicles of information to Indian librarians about technical reports.

Technical Reports can be acquired also as microforms. The chief advantages of this option are about 90 per cent saving in costs and 90 per cent saving in storage space. The chief disadvantages are the user reluctance to microfiche reports, the need of storing and air conditioning facilities, and the need of supporting user equipment. The procurement of microform technical reports in Indian libraries involves special problems because they are not normally handled in the traditional way through the channel of book trade.

Selection of Patents

A Patent is an intellectual property right (IPR) granted by the Government to exclude others from making, using, offering for sale or selling, the inventions throughout the country or importing the invention into the country for a limited time. Almost every country has a patent law and patent office to regulate matters connected with patent rights. The following passage taken from the US Patent Office website will help you to know the social purpose behind the patent system:

"The premise of our patent system lies in the mutual benefit to both the inventor and the country. The US Patent Office offers certain rights to an inventor for up to 20 years, during which time the inventor may exclude all others from making, using, importing or selling his or her invention. The patent is published and disseminated to the public so that others may study the invention and improve upon it. The constant evolution of science and technology spurred by the monetary incentives in US patent system offers to inventors, strengthens our national economy. New inventions lead

to new technologies, create new jobs, and improve our quality of life." (*www..uspto.gov/*).

In a science library, particularly in an industrial library supporting R&D activities, the importance and relevance of a patent collection cannot be questioned. Relevant patents and their specifications are acquired and kept for use. Patent searches are often undertaken to identify and locate relevant patents or for knowing whether a particular invention has been already patented. In India the procurement of patents has been greatly facilitated by the Gov. of India Ministry of Commerce through its Office of the Patent Information System (PIS) at Nagpur. This was established in 1980 with the objective of: (a) obtaining and maintaining a comprehensive collection of patent specifications and patent related literature on a worldwide basis, (b) facilitating patent searches, and (c) providing Patent Documentation Full Text, and other patent related information services. Besides the PIS in Nagpur, the National Science Library (NSL), New Delhi has very vast patent databases. NSL provides access to its international patent databases viz. *Derwent Innovations Index* (DII), *Delhphion*, WIPS, Questal, etc. The DII provides web access to patent records with links to the cited and citing patents, cited articles, and full text patent data sources in the Chemical Sciences, Electrical and Electronics, and Engineering - all from 1963 to the present. One can search more than 14.6 million patent records by topic, inventor, patent number and more. The WIPS (Worldwide Intellectual Property Search) databases provide online patent search services from worldwide databases of US, Europe (Switzerland, Germany, France, and UK), Japan, Korea, China and other International Patent Documentation Centres.

DIGITAL INFORMATION

The availability of and facilities for accessing digital information is at present also a major factor governing collection development programme in special libraries / information centres. We are in a Digital Age now. 'Digital Age' is an expression used to mean the present information environment in which more and more information and information sources are made available in the digital form either for online use or offline use. The recent developments in electronics, computers and communication have made possible the recording, transmitting and accessing of knowledge and information in a variety of digital forms, like texts, still or moving images, sound, and their combinations. In the matter of collection building Digital Age provides alternatives or options in procuring and keeping information sources. The new possibilities are: either to go for an exclusively digital library collection, or to have both traditional library materials and digitized documents side by side (a hybrid collection).

Electronic Databases

Collection Development in science libraries particularly has become very complex due to the fast emergence of new technologies in document formats during the last few decades. They range from offline sources like CD-ROM, to a wide variety of online sources, like Online databases, e-Books, e-Journals, e-Newspapers, Full-Text (aggregated) databases, indexing and abstracting databases, Reference databases (like biographies, dictionaries, directories, encyclopedias, etc.), Numeric and Statistical databases, e-images, and e-audio-visual resources. Even the Internet services in general and the World Wide Web are vast sources of digital information, like online library catalogues, bibliographies/databases, subject specific portals, subject gateways, web pages of institutions, professional bodies, conferences and congresses, personal web pages and blogs, listserv, discussion groups, etc. On the whole the expression 'electronic resources' refers to those materials that require some computer access, whether through a personal computer, main frame, or handheld mobile service.

These materials may be either accessed remotely via the internet or locally as in the case with a CD-ROM or similar offline digital information packages. E-resources present a number of challenges not encountered with the selection and acquisition of traditional analog materials, and it is advisable for the library to develop clear policies and processes for the selection and management of such resources. The main considerations in acquiring e-resources should be not only cost and convenience, but also their technical feasibility, functionality and reliability, vendor support, supply including pricing models, and licensing considerations. Librarians have to be familiar with guidelines issued by professional bodies on this subject. For example, the IFLA document entitled *Key Issues for e-resources collection development: a guide for libraries, ed. by* Sharon Johnson, et al. (Aug 2012) is perhaps the latest that can be pointed out. An earlier one brought out by the American Library Association, namely *Guidelines for the introduction of electronic information resources to users,* prepared for the Reference and User Services Association of the ALA, (revised in 2006), generally known as the 'RUSA Guidelines', is also useful.

Librarians have to be familiar with the major vendors or providers of electronic databases as well as the main databases that are useful to the scientific community. All electronic databases are not alike: some are bibliographic while some others are textual, some are subject specific but others are multidisciplinary, and some are free databases while all others are to be paid. Recently, more and more electronic journals are being published as 'open access journals' in the sense that they are freely accessible online. In the same manner there are also open access databases. We can look up for a directory of such journals (DOAJ) on the net.

A list of all available electronic databases (of academic & scientific journals) can be obtained from the net. The following is a list of some of the databases that are useful for a science library:

- *Aerospace & High Technology Database (ProQuest)*
- *AGRICOLA* (US-NAL)
- *AGRIS* (FAO/UN)
- *Analytical Abstracts* (Royal Soc. of Chem)
- *Analytical Science Digital Library*
- *Association for Computing Machinery Digital Library*
- *Astrophysics Data Systems (Harv.Univ)*
- *Beilstein database (Elsevier)*
- *Bilogical Abstracts* (Thomson Reuters)
- *BioOne*
- *Bioinformatic Harvester*
- *Business & Industry (FirstSearch)*
- *Business Dateline (FirstSearach)*
- *Business Source Premier (EBSCO)*
- *CAB Abstracts*
- *ChemXSeer*
- *Chemical Abstracts Services*
- *Citebase Search*
- *CiteSeerX*
- *Computer Database (Gale)*
- *Current Contents*
- *Digital Library for Earth System Education (DLESE)*
- *EnergyFile (OSTI/DDE)*
- *EMBASE*
- *Food Science & Technology Abstracts*
- *Compendex*
- *GEOBASE (FirstSearach)*
- *GreenFILE (EBSCO)*
- *GoPubMed*
- *IEEExplore*
- *Index Copernicus*
- *Indian Citation Index*
- *InfoTrac Agriculture Collection (Gale)*
- *InfoTrac General Science Collection (Gale)*

- *InfoTrac Nursing and Allied Health Collection (Gale)*
- *InfoTrac Environmental Issues & Policy Collection (Gale)*
- *Ingenta Connect*
- *Inspec*
- *J-STOR*
- *MathSciNET*
- *Medline Plus (FirstSearch)*
- *Merck Index*
- *Meteorological and Geophysical Abstracts*
- *National Library of Medicine*
- *National Science Digital Libarary*
- *ProQuest Biology Journals*
- *ProQuest Computing Journals*
- *ProQuest Health Management Journals*
- *ProQuest Nursing & Allied Health Sciences*
- *ProQuest Science Journals*
- *PubMed*
- *PubChem*
- *Science.gov*
- *Science Citation Index*
- *SCIRUS*
- *SPIRES-HEP*
- *Springer-Link*
- *Toxnet*
- *Web of Science*
- *WorldCat*
- *WorldWide Science*
- *The Zoological Record*

Many of the important academic and scientific databases are being provided by commercial bodies. Some of the major providers of electronic databases are listed below:

Fig. 6.3. List of Major Electronic Databases In Science

- EDBSCO
- EMERALD
- FirstSearch
- Gale
- Project Muse
- ProQuest
- ScienceDirect
- Springer Link
- Taylor and Francis

Fig. 6.4. Major Electronic Database Providers

Networks & Consortia

Collection development in the present networked environment is a more complex task than earlier as there are more choices for information professionals, between paper-based and electronic formats, between purchasing, licensing and borrowing options. One major option now available to libraries is participation in consortia. A consortium is an association of two or more institutions with the objective of participating in a common activity or pooling their resources for achieving a common goal. Based on this concept many library consortia have come to be established all over the world. Several such initiatives have already come into operation in our country. The following is a list of the major on-going library consortia in India:

- *CERA (Consortium for e-Resources in Agriculture,* (IARI, Pusa, New Delhi).
- *CSIR Library Consortium* (NISC AIR)
- *DAE Library Consortium for Scientific Research* (Department of Atomic Energy Library Consortia).
- *FORSA Consortium* (Forum for Resource Sharing in Astronomy and Astrophysics).
- *HELINET (Health Sciences Library & Information Network*) (Rajiv Gandhi University of Health Sciences, Bangaluru).

- *ICICI Knowledge Park Library Consortia* (Industrial Credit and Investment Corporation of India, Hyderabad).
- ICMR Library Consortium
- *IIM's Library Consortia* (Indian Institutes of Management)
- *INDEST Consortium - Indian National Digital Library in Engineering Sciences and Technology* (MHRD, IIT Delhi).
- ISRO Library Consortium
- *UGC-INFONET Consortia* (INFLIBNET, Ahmedabad).

Fig. 6.5. List of the Major on-going Library Cosortia in India

However, the two national level consortia are worth special mention here. For academic libraries in India, the UGC-INFOTEL Consortium is there, while for Science, Technology, and Management educational institutions the AICTE-INDEST Consortium is available. Both are being widely used by libraries today. For libraries having membership in the consortium, electronic journals and databases coming under the scope of that consortium can be subscribed to at the consortium prices which will be very low compared to their normal prices. The attached list of items covered by the UGC-INFOTEL Consortium and the AICTE-INDEST Consortium can be of help in taking appropriate decisions with respect to participating in the Consortium and benefitting from that.

A. UGC-INFONET DIGITAL LIBRARY CONSORTIUM

Full-Text e- Resources : (No. of journals covered are indicated in brackets).

- *American Chemical Society (37)*
- *American Institute of Physics (18)*
- *American Physical Society (10)*
- *Annual Reviews (33)*
- *Blackwell Publishing (497)*
- *Cambridge University Press (234)*
- *Elsevier Science (34)*

- *Emerald (Library Science Collection) (29)*
- *Institute of Physics (46)*
- *J-STOR (1,401)*
- *Nature (1)*
- *Oxford University Press (202)*
- *Portland Press (8)*
- *Project Euclid (23)*
- *Project Muse (407)*
- *Royal Society of Chemistry(29)*
- *STAM (14)*
- *Springer Link (1,950)*
- *Taylor & Francis (1,076)*

Bibliographical Databases

- *SciFinder Scholar*
- *MathScinet*
- *Royal Society of Chemistry (6 databases)*
- *ISID*
- *JCCC*
- *Chemical Abstracts Service*
- *Biological Abstracts*

B. INDEST – AICTE CONSORTIUM

Full-Text e-Resources

- *ABI/Inform*
- *ACM Digital Library*
- *ASCE Journals*
- *ASME Journals*
- *Capitaline*
- *EBSCO host*
- *Elsevier Science Digest*
- *Emerald Complete*
- *L.E.L. Online*
- *Nature*
- *Proquest Science*
- *Springer Verlag Journals*
- *Web of Science*

Bibliographical Databases

- *Chemical Abstracts Service*
- *Compendex*
- *INSPEC*
- *JCCC*
- *MathScinet*
- *SciFinder Scholar*

Fig. 6.6. List Of E-resources Covered By Two Major Consortia

Digital Libraries

A fast developing phenomenon in the library and information scenario at present is the digitization of original print and other formats. Digital libraries are now almost permanent sources of many original documents which might be otherwise unavailable for reading or reference, If at all they are available somewhere they are location bound. But digital libraries make them universally accessible at all times in all locations. In India also many libraries are undertaking the task of digitizing some category of materials or the other. The National Science Library in the Indian Institute of Science, Bangaluru has taken up the Digital Library of India Project with the objective of digitizing 1 million books by 2005. The Traditional Knowledge Digital Library (TKDL) of the Govt. of India is another important project intended at digitizing source documents of indigenous medicine. The National Library of India, Calcutta also has its own digitization project. The *Vidyanidhi* Project of the University of Mysore is digitizing Ph.D. theses. The INFLIBNET has a similar project on a wider scale. Even in Kerala several digitization initiatives have been reported. The most important one in Kerala is the digital library project of the State Central Library, Trivandrum which has already accomplished more than 1.2 million pages of printed matter, covering over 1,200 rare books and copies of the Government Gazette from 1903-1954.

The following are some of the important digital library projects of the world:

- Google Books (12 million +)
- Europeana (10 million + objects)
- Hathi Trust (10million +)
- WikiSource (3.5 million +)
- Internet Archive (3.1 million +)
- Universal Digital Library (1.5 million +)
- Open Library (1 million +)
- Digital Library of India (325,473 vols,)
- Project Gutenberg (38,000 +)

Fig. 6.7. List of Major Digital Library Projects of the World

Collection development must be in direct response to our knowledge of both the needs of the user community and the information sources that are available for collecting. A good collection can be developed only through proper collection management policies, and this in turn will be a reflection of the mission and objectives of the wider organization we are called upon to serve. The formulation of the Collection Development Policy Statement which defines the overall aim of the policy and the procedures that are involved in achieving this aim has a crucial role in collection development. We have given in this section all the necessary guidelines for these in the context of a science library. Other factors that can influence collection development, like the growth of the digital information, the availability of electronic databases, the network and consortia environment available, the emergence of digital libraries, etc. are also explained. We are getting also necessary knowledge about the various selection tools and aids for books generally, and periodicals, technical reports, and patents, particularly. We have given here a list of important databases, the major providers, and the titles covered by the UGC-INFONET and the INDEST-AICTE Consortia. These will surely have practical use for anyone as a science librarian.

TECHNICAL ORGANIZATION OF THE COLLECTION

Once materials began to be acquired steps have to be taken for the technical organization of the collection. The purpose of technical organization is to make ready the collection for the convenience of the readers as well as of the staff. For this, the collection has to be so organized as to help in:

(a) knowing whatever that are available in the library;

(b) locating whatever are wanted; and

(c) arranging materials in the most helpful order for facilitating both (a) and (b) above.

Traditional Library Practices

In a traditional library set up technical organization is mainly confined to facilitating storage and retrieval of documents. This involves mainly three things:

1. Classification as a tool in organizing the collection based on the specific subjects dealt with in each document;
2. **Cataloguing** as a tool to access and retrieve the specific documents; and
3. **Shelf arrangement** as a method of exposing the documents for facilitating easy location of the required documents.

The Science Library is a special library and in respect of all the three matters listed above there are differences between a general library (academic or public) and a special library. The following table will help to understand those differences:

	General Library	***Special Library***
Documents	Macro documents: viz. Books, Monographs, Bound Volumes of Periodicals, etc.	Micro-documents: viz. Reports, Standards, Patents, Specifications, Multimedia items, etc.
Subjects	General Macro subjects	Specialized micro subjects

Classification	General & broad schemes	Special & in-depth schedules
Cataloguing	Brief & Non-descriptive	Detailed & descriptive
Media & Format	Mainly print materials	Print materials plus multimedia & digital items

Fig. 6.8. Table showing Differences Between a General Library and a Special Library

Changing trends

In the overall library scenario of today we can notice many new trends in technical organization. They can be listed here:

- Modern libraries are moving towards computerized cataloguing;
- Many libraries engage in retrospective catalogue conversion into computer readable form;
- There is increasing use of on-line cataloguing;
- Many use online catalogue databases for down-loading entries;
- Creation of short title catalogues is adopted in clearing back logs;
- Libraries fulfill their network obligations and upload local databases into networks;
- Decreasing importance of classification for assigning individualizing Class Numbers and arranging them in the classified order;
- Use of Class Numbers as only location symbols for documents (as physical units);
- Use of specific subject headings and thesauri for identification and accessing of information / documents;
- De-professionalization of cataloguing, in the sense that qualified librarians are no more essential in doing cataloguing work.

Choice of a Classification Scheme

In spite of the on-going changes in trends one thing that still persists in modern libraries is Library Classification. The choice of a classification scheme is crucially important. The use of this scheme is primarily in assigning a Call Number to each book, or such other document, so as to fix its relative position in the sequential arrangement on shelves. In the modern context it is imperative that the classification scheme chosen must have a Notation system that is amenable to computerization. One may ask: why should there be a classified arrangement at all?

Some advantages of a classification scheme cannot be just overlooked. Firstly, it gives a logical and filiatory sequence, either of books on the shelves (in an open access collection) or their surrogates in the catalogue or database. Secondly, when classification is used in an information system the recall and precision in the retrieval of information will become the most favourable. This feature will be found more dominant in analytico-synthetic schemes such as the UDC and the CC.

Choice of a Catalogue Code

Next to the choice of a classification scheme comes the choice of a Catalogue code. Relative merits and demerits of different catalogue codes have to be examined. Whether to use the Classified Catalogue Code (CCC) or the AACR? Whether to go for descriptive cataloging or not?, and the use of the MARC format or the Common Communication Format (CCF)? – these are some of the major issues involved. Our final decision has to depend upon the compatibility of the chosen Code and Format to computerization. New options are also now available. For example, catalogue data can be downloaded from online sources like the *OCLC WorldCat*, the *Library Congress Catalogue*, etc. provided that our software is fully compatible to this specific task.

Choice of a Library Software

There are ever so many library application software packages now in the market. Each one may have its own advantages and disadvantages. The choice of the right software is therefore a serious issue.

The recent trend is not in favour of high priced commercial software. At least in India, Government organizations have taken initiatives in developing or sponsoring inexpensive software packages for libraries like the KOHA and the e-Grandhalaya. Both these are open source software and are integrated system packages that provide modules for bibliographical database building as well as for the various household operations of a library or an information system. One significant and essential component of the chosen software package should be the OPAC (Online Public Access Catalogue) module with provision for local configuration and customization as well the technology for WebOPAC. Another essential feature must be the protocol for downloading catalogue data from online catalogues. Both *KOHA* and *e-Grandhalaya* have the above two features. Professional associations or university departments in LIS are now-a-days conducting necessary training programmes in both the above mentioned library software packages.

Integrated Systems and Technologies

The choice of the library software has to be in due regard to the needs of an integrated systems and technologies that present day libraries warrant. Until 1990s, an 'integrated system' was considered to be one that computerizes a multiplicity of library functions using one common database. But the scope and potential of today's systems have far exceeded such a limited vision. They now provide much more than a common database for both the users and librarians. Some of the qualities of the systems that libraries now expect are:

- Comprehensive connectivity to all kinds of systems, including older, 'legacy' systems;
- The ability to establish and control external links to remote resources;
- The ability to customize the system locally;
- Seamless movement between and among functions within the systems;
- Search engine power and flexibility;
- Support for all recognized standards; and
- Compatibility with the World Wide Web.

The following passage from the book of John M. Cohn, et. al.(2002) almost fully brings out the purpose and scope of integrated systems and technologies in libraries and information centres:

> *"The purpose and scope of the library's automated, integrated system was broadened to do more than just computerize manual or paper-based routines. Systems had to connect through the local library or network of libraries, into systems of other vendors, far-flung networks, full-content databases, and, of course, the Internet. 'Accessibility' was redefined to include the ability to obtain resources and information in all formats wherever it was located, from anywhere, at any time, day or night. Thus, 'automating the library' no longer refers only to computerizing operations in a discrete, physical place. It has assumed a wider frame of reference – namely that of enabling the library user to reach beyond what is 'merely' local, to an information and knowledge base that is truly global and inter connected".*

Therefore, it is very much necessary to strategically plan for the introduction of a set of integrated systems and technologies.

Storage and Display of Materials

The results of technical organization will be revealed only when the documents of different types are duly arranged and displayed on shelves or in whatever other storage media. The treatments given to different species of documents will vary. While books are kept on shelves, current issues of periodicals are kept on display racks and their completed volumes are given proper binding and thereafter treated similar to books and shelved for use. Research reports, Patents, Specifications, Standards, etc. are arranged in vertical files, or pamphlet boxes or specially made box files. Similarly, filmed, processed and digital materials, like microfilms and fiche, CD-ROMs, DVDs, computer diskettes, cassettes, etc have to be given appropriate storages.

In this Section we have explained all the issues connected with the technical organization and storage of the materials acquired by the library so as to help both the library users and the library staff to know whatever that are available in the library and to facilitate the location, retrieval and use of whatever that are required. Unlike in the past modern libraries are using more of information technology in the technical organization of the documents. However the storage and display of the materials in their physical formats are also equally important with the technical organization.

CONCLUSION

In the forgoing chapter we have covered three different topics, namely Information Sources, Collection Development, and Technical Organization. Regarding the first, we have given almost an elaborate listing of the categories of information sources now available. In the section on Collection Development we have given an exposure to the principles and factors governing good collection building activity. Collection involves selection and therefore the tools and aids in selecting the right materials are described in detail. The case of digital information has been almost comprehensively dealt with including the major electronic databases available, the on-going library consortia in India, and major digital library initiatives. The lists given here are not claimed to be complete or up to date. Nevertheless, they will help anyone to get a full view of the overall situation. Finally, at this point, we hope, that one is pretty familiar with all aspects of building up and developing a purposive collection for any science library or information system when called upon to manage.

In the end we have discussed the Technical organization of the collection with due emphasis on the introduction of an Integrated System Technologies.

REFERENCES

AMERICAN LIBRARY ASSOCIATION (1996), *Guide for training collection development librarians* (quoted in John Kennedy, *Collection Management, A Concise Introduction,* Woodhead Publishing Limited, 2006 (*www.sciencedirect.com*)

AMERICAN LIBRARY ASSOCIATION (2006), *Guidelines for the introduction of electronic information resources to users*, prepared for the Reference and User Services Association of the ALA, (revised in 2006).

ATHERTON, Pauline. *Handbook for information systems and services*, Paris, UNESCO, 1977.

BHATTACHARYYA, G. (1982) "Some of the basic principles of Library Science based on the Five Laws of Library /Science" *Library Science with a Slant to Documentation*, 1982. DRTC, Bangalore.

BONNE, George S. (1971)."Chapter 2 Information Sources" *shodhganga,inflibnet,ac,in* downloaded on 18/08/2020

COHN, John M, et. al.(2002), *Planning for integrated systems and technologies; a how-to-do-it Manual for librarians,* edn. 2. London, Facet Publishing, 2002.

EVANS, E.G. *Management techniques for libraries*, 1976

GREGORY, Vicki L. *Collection development and management for 21st century collections: an introduction,* London, Neal-Schuman Publishers, 2011.

IFLA (2012), *Key Issues for e-resources collection development: a guide for libraries, ed. by* Sharon Johnson, et al. (Aug 2012)

JOHNSON, Peggy (2004), *Fundamentals of Collection Development and Management*, Chicago, American Library Association,2004 342 p.

PATENT SYSTEM OF U.S.." (*www..uspto.gov/*).

RANGANATHAN, S.R. *Library administration, Ed. 2,* Bombay, Asia Publishing House, 1959.

SEETHARAMA, S. *Guidelines for planning of libraries and information centres,* Calcutta, IASLIC, 1990.

SPILLER, David. *Providing materials for library users*. London, Library Association, 2000.

SRIDHAR, M .S. *Problems of Collection Development in Special Libraries,* New Delhi, Concept Publications, 1992.

VARSHNEY, Anamika (2011) *Sources of Information* LIS BD Network, Library & Information Science Academic Blog *www.lisbdnet.com* downloaded on 16/08/2020

7
Information Products and Services

Generation of appropriate information products and services should be the ultimate concern of all those who are planning a science information system, and every other knowledge that is acquired in that connection is only by way of preparing for or facilitating this end. One must be able to do a portfolio analysis of the information services department which he has to manage. Generally, all information services can fall into 4 broad categories: Reference Services, Current Awareness Services, Information Analysis Services, and Supporting Services. A detailed analysis of each of these four categories of services will be useful and relevant.

REFERNCE SERVICES

Reference Services in a Science Library may include the following:

- Answering queries (= Ready Reference Service);
- Readers' Guidance (= Instruction and guidance in the choice of the right documents);
- Referral Services (= Query transfers to other libraries in the case of a Long Range Reference Service);

- Literature Searches (= Compilng of retrospective documentation lists).

CURRENT AWARENESS SERVICES

Current Awareness Services (CAS) may include the following:

- Notifying current information (like, Current Titles List, Article/Book Alert Services, etc);
- Research in Progress Bulletin
- SDI (Selective Dissemination of Information) Services
- Newspaper Clipping Service
- Announcement Services, like:
  - Notification of Contracts
  - Products Information Bulletin
  - Process Information Bulletin
  - Patent Information
  - Standards Information
  - New innovations
  - Technology Transfer Information
  - Notification about Conferences /Meetings/ Symposia

INFORMATION ANALYSIS SERVICES

This category of services has different options.

The Services include:

- Indexing
- Abstracting
- Extraction
- Evaluation

The products are various and include:

- Indexing / abstracting bulletins

- Condensations, Compilations and Evaluations
- Critical Compilations
- State of the Art Reports
- Forecasts & Trend Reports
- Techno-economic Surveys
- Information Packages for Small Entrepreneurs
- Special Services to Top Management, like:
  - MIS (Management Information System)
  - Commercial Intelligence & Information
  - Market Intelligence & Information
  - Forecasts and trend notes
  - Company profiles
- Environmental Information, like:
  - Regulatory / legal
  - Political
  - Economic
  - Social
  - Technological
  - Digests for technical divisions
  - Digests for Operators / technicians
  - Technical Notes
  - Data banks and data service

COMMON SUPPORTING SERVICES

The two Common Supporting Services are:

- Translation Services, and
- Reprography Service

These are explained below:

Translation Service : Librarians of science libraries must know the fact that 50% of the world's scientific and technical literature is published not in the English language, while German, Danish, Russian, French and Japanese are the other main languages having engineering literature. These non-English publications do contain useful information. Hence, translation is an essential interface between foreign language documents and readers. Every library ought to have made prior arrangements for providing translation services. There can be ad hoc translation services, as well as regular translation services, both on request and in anticipation. There can be full-time translators on the staff of the library, or arrangements can be made with a panel of ad hoc translators outside of the library. Alternatively, as and when needed the library can take the services and facilities of regional and national documentation centres, like the NISCAIR. There are translation centres and translation banks where already translated items are available. One must be familiar with different national and international arrangements already available, including also the efforts at bibliographical control of translated documents.

The BLLD (British Library Lending Division) Translations Service has three components, namely translation of individual periodical articles, cover to cover translation of whole journals, and translation of books. The system has already a large stock of translated individual items, complete runs of at least 250 cover to cover journals, as well as ad hoc translation of selected papers. In USA, the National Translation Centre (NTC) in Chicago has the largest collection of translations in that country. The European Translation Centre (ETC) in Delft (Netherlands) of the European Productivity Agency, is another such example. In India, the INSDOC (under NISCAIR) has its own large scale translation programmes including responsive translations and regular inter-governmental programmes under bilateral treaties. INSDOC maintains a national roster of translators by which translations from any language text can be arranged and supplied in a very reasonable time. There are also important bibliographic sources for translated materials, like the *BLLD Announcement Bulletin* and the *BLLD Review*, the *Commonwealth Index of Unpublished Scientific and Technical Translations* (ASLIB), the *Translation Register Index* of the US National Translation Centre, the *World Index of Scientific Translations* (monthly, quarterly and annual) of the European Translation Centre (ETC), the *National Index of Translations* (INSDOC), etc.

Reprography Services : This is to be viewed as a crucial part of the total document delivery system. Libraries may give options like in-house consultation, home lending, acquiring on inter-library loans, supply of photocopies, microfilms/fiche, digital copies, etc. The special advantages that reprography provides for science libraries / information centres are:

1. Procuring copies of out-of-print or unpublished material;
2. Securing the contents of valuable documents;
3. Publishing in limited copies using the 'in-house publishing' option;
4. Saving of storage space in the library,
5. Cost saving by excluding purchase of a whole document, etc.

SOME SPECIALLY ASSIGNED SERVICES

Librarians in special libraries are often assigned some special responsibilities and services for which they are supposed to be endowed with necessary qualities, qualifications, competence and skills. The following are these special assignments:

- Organizing Exhibitions
- Organizing Seminars, Workshops, etc.
- Editorial & Technical Writing Services
- Preparation of Charts, Maps, Slides, etc. for Displays and Presentations.

- Liaison Service

Organizing Exhibitions

Exhibition has been an important item in the traditional Library extension and publicity methods. In a science library environment, especially in an industrial library, this is a specialty in which the librarian / information centre manager is expected to be competent and resourceful. The selection of the theme, the exhibits, displays of the exhibits, etc. could be better done by the librarian than anybody else in the organization as he/ she only has more intimate knowledge of both the items and their potential users.

Organizing Seminars, Workshops, etc.

This is another area in which Librarians' multi-faceted abilities are reckoned with. They will be competent to handle many of the procedural and practical problems involved in organizing and conducting seminars and workshops. Right from the generation of the idea and submitting the original proposal, announcing the seminars, fixing the venues, inviting participation, call for papers, receiving and processing abstracts and full texts of papers, printing and production of the pre-seminar volume, arranging hospitality including transportation, accommodation, and food, providing computer and database support at venue of the seminar – there are ever so many items of jobs and responsibilities involved in the conduct of seminars and workshops. In all these matters a resourceful Librarian and staff can play a meritorious role. In some cases at least they will be getting the co-operation and support of the P.R.O and his Department in this whole endeavour.

Editorial and Technical Writing Services

Very often, Science Librarians will be called upon to shoulder ever so many extra library activities. One such thing is the responsibility with respect to Editorial and Technical

Writing. This is because, of all people in the organization, Librarian is perhaps the one with the general competency and infrastructural facilities at command including a close knit team of staff to share the work. Several activities are generally involved here, like:

(a) Preparation of scientific and technical write-ups on demand for publishing in learned periodicals and other media;

(b) Popular write-ups for mass media like newspapers, popular science periodicals, brochures, etc.

(c) Compilation of periodical S &T Progress Reports;

(d) Compilation and preparation of Process and Product Reports based on know-how generated 'in-house';

(e) Compilation, editing and preparation of conference and seminar proceedings;

(f) Publishing of miscellaneous materials like leaflets, brochures, newsletters, house journals, etc.

(g) Miscellaneous responsibilities like proof correction, lay-out design of print materials, etc.

Preparation of Charts, Maps, Presentations, etc.

This is another area that involves expertise, experience and soft skills, which some librarians and information professionals at least can acquire and develop. Having been equipped with the necessary infrastructure, for example, computers, net facilities, laser printers, scanners, etc. Librarians can volunteer to give proper Presentation support (Power Point for example) to scientists and executives who have to participate in conferences, seminars, workshops, etc. Such services will be duly recognized and will boost up the image of library / information profession.

Liaison Service

In the specific context of a library / information centre

which is supporting an industrial or business enterprise Librarian will have to function almost as a liaison officer between the parent organization and other bodies, institutions or individuals with whom the parent organization has dealings. Librarian must be able to study the background, infrastructure, and interests of enterprises and individuals concerned and visualize the ways in which they can be connected with the organization and library programmes and services. Some of the other responsibilities of a liaison nature are listed below:

- Learning about and collecting data and information on the future plans of other companies.
- Developing appropriate programmes to provide information support for the specific plans of one's own company.
- Identifying experts in business, R & D, and other institutions for consultation as and when necessary;
- Promoting contacts with enterprises having similar interests, projects and programmes, between industries and R&D institutions;
- Visiting the organizations outside;
- Attending conferences, seminars, meetings, etc. with Information Centre staff and those in the industry.

SOCIAL MEDIA & E-DELIVERY OF SERVICES

With the recent advancements in ICT many new possibilities are open for libraries in their service delivery. Web sites, e-mails, bulletin boards, etc. are already familiar to librarians. The emergence of Web 2.0 technology with its social networking tools has been a great promise for librarians as they can now interact with their users to study their individualistic needs and give a useful feedback. As one may know, Web 2.0 is the collection of server-based solutions that have allowed the web to become a publishing platform. Instead of the traditional way of web authoring, Web 2.0 solutions invite all Internet users to share, collaborate and contribute in the website development process. These Web 2.0 based solutions are generally referred to as either "social media" or "social networking".

Thus, the term "Social Networking" refers to a range of web-enabled software programs that allow users to interact and work collaboratively with other users. The users can browse, search, invite friends to connect and interconnect, share views, commend, hold discussions, post blog entries, describe events, videos, music, and more. A social network allows an individual to join and create a personal profile, then formally connect with other users of the system as social friends. There are several social connecting sites now in the Web 2.0 domain, like the FaceBook, MySpace, Twitter, YouTube, etc. The exponential growth of social media has made it inevitable for librarians to learn to use these tools to serve their IT-enriched patrons on their same footing, but in a more individualistic, interactive, specialized and value added way. This has led to the development of Library 2.0 which is a buzzword now. The concept has been borrowed from Web 2.0 and follows similar philosophies.

Library 2.0 has been defined as "the application of interactive, collaborative and multimedia web-based technologies to web-based library services and collections" (Mishra, 2008) This is a paradigm shift of the library in the internet epoch. Librarians must begin to use this Web 2.0 application if they want to prove themselves just as relevant as other information providers, and start delivering experiences that meet the expectation of the user in this fast changing information environment.

Many different programs are now available and being used for social networking, each one may be specially useful for specific types of communication and interaction, like the following:

Facebook & Myspace : used for social networking, i.e. connecting single user with hub of friends.

Ning : used for initiating discussions on subjects of topical interest with members of an association, etc

LinkedIn : used for connecting users with experts in their chosen fields of interest.

Blog & Twiitter : used for blogging, i.e. personal authoring and publishing, updating on activities and programmes.

Wiki : used for Collaborative authoring, i.e. Open editing and Tagging.

Podcasting : used for multimedia authoring and syndication.

YouTube & Google : used for video collections and video uploading.

Flickr : used for photo and image management; Open Image Access and Tagging.

LibraryThing & Lib.rario.us & Del.icio.us &Tagging : These are used for social cataloguing and tracking of books, media, etc. and for bookmarking. Tagging is used for adding keywords to any digital object.

RSS (Really Simple Syndication) : used for syndicating content from blogs or web pages; it summarizes information items and links them to the information sources.

Social Networking under the Web 2.0 and the Library 2.0 technology has brought to front enormous possibilities of serving clients. The traditional approach to service delivery where the library passes information to its patrons without feedback will no longer suffice for our new generation clients. In fact, library users have been yearning to be part of the services rendered to them by being able to dictate what they need and thereby causing a more interactive service delivery which will foster a two way communication pathway. Social networking tool is a platform where users are both consumers and creators of online content. In this platform librarian can constantly evaluate and update the contents of his products to meet the changing needs of users, with the collaboration and sharing of ideas by the patrons. Encouraging users' participation and feedback are crucial in the development and maintenance of quality services. Social networking sites will allow librarians to adopt a new role by placing themselves in a social realm with users. By reading blogs, group postings, and message boards, the librarian becomes an active participant who is able to guide and advise patrons as needs arise. Today, many enterprising librarians, not only in developed countries but also in developing countries, have gone ahead with innovative services through the social media platforms. For example, in Nigeria (Ezeani, 2012) librarians use different Social Networking sites as described below:

Facebook : This is the most popular of the social networking sites used in libraries, because it s the most librarian-friendly with its many applications like the J-STOR and WorldCat search.

MySpace : In academic institutions libraries can use this site to post calendars, custom catalogue search tools, and blog features to improve services.

Blogs : Librarians can periodically post messages, share information on a particular subject or issues, and allow users to contribute to content. They can even write articles, news on topical issues, and expect an instant reaction from their users.

Wikis : This, as we know, is a free online encyclopedia which offers platform for users to access, edit and contribute content. This is a collaborative endeavour for developing web content.

LinkedIn : Librarians can get patrons connected with specialists in their particular fields of interest via LinkedIn. Librarian can also use this platform to render specialized services to patrons, like the SDI.

Twitter : This micro blogging application can be used to keep library staff and patrons updated on daily activities, like frequently updated collections. Users can utilize this platform to write short messages or status updates. They can also send Instant Messages on complaints or ask questions on a particular issue and get a feedback on the spot using the twitter.

YouTube : Events, such as conferences, seminars and workshops can be disseminated via the YouTube with video clippings of important highlights of inaugural functions, lectures, deliberations, etc.

Ning : Librarians can get connected with users, library associations, etc. via Ning. The Nigerian Library Association uses this platform to discuss topical issues among the members.

Flickr : Librarians can use this tool to share, distribute new images of library collections, cover pages of new books and journals received, etc. In Nigeria, it is used by libraries to enlighten users on topical issues such as national elections, contesting political parties and candidates.

LibraryThing : This is a tool that can enrich the library OPAC. Once an account is created, a list of books with their ISBNs is sent to Library Thing which sends back a piece of code which is posted into the footer of the Library OPAC. Librarians can utilize this to send a list of current publications to users.

The following remarks from the Nigerian Librarian is worthy of your special attention:

> *"The concept of a library as a physical place where one can visit to get information is rapidly changing to a social cyberspace where users across, communicate and contribute to existing knowledge. This is because the modern library of the 21st century is characterized with collective knowledge creation and enabling technologies, and also a movement away from, the old*

stereotype, conventional and one directional library services to users, to a more dynamic, two-way communicated networkenvironment characterized by open access content creation, collaborative and participatory social space where users are free to access and contribute content. The potentials of the modern technology with the Open Access Protocols provide the opportunity for free access, free interaction, free communication and contribution to knowledge" (Ezeani, 2012).

Librarians can use social networking tools in three broad activities, viz. (a) Information and communication, (b) Knowledge distribution, and (c) Knowledge organization. In the case of Information and Communication, the tools available are: MySpace, Facebook, Ning, Blog, Meebo, LinkedIn, and Twitter. In Knowledge distribution the tools relevant are: Flickr, YouTube, TeacherTube, SecondLife, Wickipedia, PBwiki, Footnote, Community Walk, Slideshare, Digg, StumpleUpon, DaftDoggy, etc. For Knowledge Organization activity librarians can use platforms like aNobii, Del.icio.us, Netvibes, Connotea, Library Thing, I, etc. (Mishra, 2008).

From the above passages one might have captured the important characteristics of Social Networking as a: Participatory, Educative, Collaborative, Fascinating, and Flexible mode of service delivery in libraries. This mode of service can be of special significance in two major areas, viz. Marketing of Information Products and Services, and Reference Services.

CHANGING TRENDS IN INFORMATION SERVICES

One will not fail to notice that in recent years the information service strategies of libraries are influenced by various environmental factors. The most obvious examples of these factors are: (a) Information and communication technology (ICT); (b) Financial and human resources; and (c) Managerial and political policies. Some changing trends in information services deserve to be listed here:

1. The range of products and services potentially available from the networked information centres differs significantly, both in qualitative and quantitative terms, from what were offered in the past.
2. Technological developments have given information service managers a wider set of options from which they can select the best mix to meet the needs of their customers. IT enabled services can be developed with improved choice, convenience and customization for individual users and groups.
3. Historically, the quality of a library was usually judged on the size of its collection of books, periodicals and other materials. Today, the emphasis has shifted from collection management to services management including the delivery of documents and other items to customers irrespective of their locations. Hence, in future, service quality will be equated more with staff competence than with collection strength.
4. Self service facilities have progressed from the traditional open-access collections and customer-operated photocopying to self–issue, returns and reservations/booking, as well as end-user database searching, downloading and printing. Online services provided by libraries can facilitate more self services.
5. Distributed delivery of centrally managed services has progressed from loans and document supply to desktop access to databases and instructional material, virtual library tours, reference desks and suggestion boxes.
6. Tailored services (often with tiered levels of provision) have been developed to meet the specific needs of particular groups, such as people with physical

disabilities or learning difficulties, and distance education students, etc.

7. The concept of a library as a physical place where one can visit to get information is rapidly changing to a social cyberspace where users across, communicate and contribute to existing knowledge.

8. Because of the emergence and growth of the knowledge-based economy where production and use of knowledge are main drivers of growth, wealth creation and employment for all industries, libraries and information centres supporting industrial establishments are being renamed as knowledge management centres. Knowledge management is a multi-disciplinary area involving besides Library & Information Science, subjects like Business and Management, and Communication and cognitive sciences, Information Technology, etc. Accordingly, the skills and competencies required of people to function as knowledge management professionals are very different from those of the traditional librarians. The names of industrial library positions are also changing, like Chief Knowledge Officer (CKO), Knowledge Engineer (KE), Chief Information Officer (CIO), Chief Technology Officer (CTO), etc.

CONCLUSION

In this chapter we have given a detailed exposure to the variety of information services one can think of organizing in a science library / information centre. Although there are many possible types of services, what is probable, positively required and feasible will vary from library to library. This has to be found out by conducting a referendum among potential users, with a full list of possible services / products and space for individuals from different user groups to mark their choices. In an industrial library four different categories of users can be visualized: (a) Top managers/ policy makers, (b) R & D staff, (c) Middle managers, and (d) workers. The products / services that each of these categories may choose will be different. When each potential user is marking his/ her choice against each item the librarian will be in a position to count the scores for each product / service and decide what is important for whom and thereby set his strategies and priorities. A special area that has been dealt with in detail in this unit is the social networking opportunities now available to librarians to make their services more participatory, fascinating and sophisticated for modern users.

REFERNCES

CORRALL, Sheila and BREWERTON (1999), Antony, *The new professional's handbook; your guide to information services.* London, Library Association, 1999.

EZEANI, Chinwe Nwogo and IGWESI, Uzoamaka (2012),"Using social media for dynamic library service delivery; the Nigerian experience" *Library philosophy and practice (e-journal)* 2012 paper no. 814 *.http://digitalcommons.unl.edu/libphilprac/814*

GLADAMOSI, B.O. (2012), "Emerging challenges to effective library automation and an e-library; the case of Emanuel Alayande College of Education, Oyo, Nigeria" *Library Philosophy and Practice (e-journal), 2012; paper no.807.*

MISHRA, C.S. (CIM, Patna), (2008), *Social networking technologies in digital environment: its possible implications on libraries,* E-LIS 2008 *.Eprints.rclis.org/16844/1/Social%20networking%20Library.pdf*

PUGH, Lyndon (2000), Change management in information services, Hampshire, Gower, 2000.

SAHU, Hemant Kumar, et al. (ICCAA, Pune) (2010), *New innovative library services: moving with Web 2.0/Library 2.0 technology ; a case study*, LISA VI, Feb 14-17,2010.

SURAWEERA, S.W. (2010), "Value of social networking in libraries and information organization in Asia and Oceania" in World Library and Information Congress: 76th IFLA General Conference and Assembly, 10-15 August 2010, Gothenberg, Sweden.

8
Human Resources Planning

In the earlier chapters we have examined the different aspects in the planning of a science library/ information system, like the study of the User community and its requirements, the Information sources available, the Collection development, the Technical organization, and the Information services to be organized. Now in this chapter we will deal with an important area, namely, Human Resources /Personnel requirements.

HUMAN RESOURCES / PERSONNEL RQUIREMENTS

The expression 'personnel' is synonymous with three other terms, 'staff', 'manpower' and 'human resources'. Among all the four, perhaps, 'human resources' can be a more acceptable term than anything else as this agrees with the modern thinking that staff is to be reckoned as an important resource of any organization rather than a liability. The dictionary definition of Human Resources is "*the personnel of a business or organization, regarded as a significant asset in terms of skills and abilities" ..."the department of a business or organization that deals with the hiring, administration, and training of staff*" (Oxford Languages /Google's English Dictionary). Human resources is the set of the people who make up the workforce of an organization, business sector, industry, or economy. A narrower concept is there which is 'human capital', the knowledge which the individuals in an organization embody, However, Human Resource Management is used to be referred to as "personnel administration", but human resources focus on the people side of management, There are two real definitions of Human Resources Management; one is that it is the process of managing people in organizations in a structured and thorough manner. This means that it covers the hiring, firing, pay and perks and performance management, This first definition is the modern and traditional version more like what a personnel manager would have done back in the 1920s. The second definition is that HRM circles the ideas of management of people in organizations from a macro management perspective. like customers and competitors in a marketplace, This involves the focus on making the "employment relationship" fulfilling for both management and employees ("Human Resources Management (HRM): Definition and Concept" *www.managementstudyguide. com* Retrieved on 26-08-2020)

Now, coming to the Human Resources required for a library / information system it has to be considered under five different heads:

- professional and support staff;
- the different levels of staff;
- number of persons required in each level;
- the qualifications for each category and level; and
- the cost of employing them (salary & other costs).

All these would depend upon the quality and quantity of work to be done in each unit of the library / information centre. Therefore, the following matters are required to be considered in connection with human resources planning:

1. the present **workload** in each unit, and the extent of increase expected in the future;

2. The available **Performance Standards**, for each unit, both National / International Standards;
3. **Information technology** and its application;
4. **Type and quality of work** to be performed in each unit;
5. **Knowledge, skills and expertise** required to perform various jobs;
6. Whether **subject specialists or information specialists** for each function?
7. Categories / levels of information professionals needed, and their **qualifications**; and
8. **Salary and other benefits** required to be provided for each post.

WORK LOAD ASSESSMENT

Work load can be calculated upon the basis of:

1. the Collection development plan, and the information services/products plan; and
2. the Performance Standards.

While (1) will be indicating the size and strength of the present collection by types and number, and the annual increase estimated, (2) will indicate the phased plan for the introduction of various services and products in successive years. The annual quantum of work in each functional section of the Library/Information centre can be estimated like in:

- Procurement Section,
- Technical Section,
- Maintenance Section,
- Circulation Section,
- Periodicals Section,
- Information Services Section,
- Documentation Section, etc.

Then by using a **Staff Formula** (as the one given by Dr.

S.R. Ranganathan) or any Performance Standard for that matter, we can calculate the manpower required for each of the functional units of the library for one year.

Job Analysis & Staff Formula

According to Dr Ranganathan (*Library Administration*, ed. 2, 1959) the activities of a library can be broken into a well articulated hierarchy of operational units of work like:

- management
  - functions
    - activities
      - work blocks
        - work
          - jobs.

A **job** is an ultimate piece of work which is best done at a single stretch and whose duration is ordinarily short. A number of related jobs constitute an item of **work**, and a number of items of work would aggregate into **work blocks**, a number of work blocks make an **activity**, and several such activities will be involved in a **function**. Dr. Ranganathan's Staff Formula has later been developed further and has come to be known as the **DRTC Manpower Norm.**

The term '**Job Analysis**' was originally used by Dr Ranganathan almost in the same sense as 'system analysis' was used in later management science, wherein every activity is analyzed to identify the hierarchical sequence of events leading to its completion. (System analysis, as we may already know, is the dissection of a system into different levels of sub-systems until its ultimate components or elements are identified so as to study how they interact and work to form a coherent whole).

But, in recent LIS literature, the term 'job analysis' is found used in a totally different meaning and connotation (For example, Peter Jordan, 1987). According to him, *"a job may be defined as a collection of tasks and responsibilities making up the work of one member of staff"*. For example are the Job Listings of the American Library Association. This may be true in common parlance also. In that sense, managers find job analysis as a helpful aid in staff structuring, allocation of work, designing new jobs or redesigning existing jobs, Job evaluation, drawing up job descriptions, personnel specification, etc. However, we must not fail to note that this is only a changed meaning of the term 'job'.

Work Flow Studies

After Dr Ranganathan, several such attempts were there. Numerous workflow studies have been done in order to bring out manpower norms. In 1966 the Dept. of Expenditure of the Ministry of Finance, Govt. of India, evolved **Standards for Government Libraries** which were revised in 1968. Both INSDOC and UGC also conducted work flow studies. Later, several bodies like Indian Standards Institution, Institute of Economic Growth, Defense Science Library, Geological Survey of India, Indian Council of Agricultural Research, etc. also brought out their own Performance Standards for library and information activities.

Performance Standards

Performance standards provide the employees with specific performance expectations for each major duty. They are the observable behaviour and actions which explain how the job is to be done, plus the results that are expected for satisfactory job performance. Now-a-days, because of the increasing interests and also because of the possibilities of computerization and automation in library and information centres, the personnel requirements need be reassessed. For this to be done, we must, first of all, identify the library operations that are amenable to computerization. Some of them are well known like:

- Library catalogue,
- Information storage and retrieval,
- Documentation work including bibliographical and textual data,
- Selection, ordering and purchase of books, monographs and serials (Acquisition and Serials Control),
- Stock recording (Accessioning), and
- Stock verification, and stock maintenance operations,
- Circulation control systems (charging and discharging in lending),
- Information search services including:
  - Classification & indexing,
  - Searching, retrieving, & feedback,
  - Indexing language,
  - Consolidation, etc.
- Management Information systems including
  - Finance and Accounts,
  - Statistics and Reporting;
  - Personnel data.

These possibilities will necessarily alter the applicability of the Performance Standards formulated earlier because they were based on manual operations only. Therefore, the DRTC Bangalore took up this task of developing a new set of Performance Standards for library and information centre activities in automated environments. Based on the old Staff Formula of Dr Ranganathan they estimated by guess the standards for a computerized set up and called it "**Guesstimated Performance Standards**". These new standards are given below:

Job items	***Standard output per person***
Book acquisition section	12,000 documents in a year.
Periodical section	4,000 issues per year.
Technical Processing section	6,000 documents per year.
Circulation Section	1,500 gate hours the Circulation Counter is kept open in an year.
Reference Section.	50 queries per day.
Maintenance Section	1 person for every 100,000 documents and 1 person for every 6,000 documents added annually.
Information Service Section	1.5 man-year per type of service.
Supervisory staff	1 person for every 1,500 hours the Library / information centre Is kept open.

Fig. 8.1. Chart showing The Guesstimated Performance Standards For Automated Libraries (DRTC, Bangaluru)

Advantages of Performance Standards

What are the possible advantages of Performance Standards? The following are worth mentioning: Performance Standards can provide an objective basis for decisions to be taken in manpower planning and controlling activities in a library or information centre. They give a factual basis for balancing the work load with personnel. They help in the choice of a cost efficient method or procedure. They aid in predicting the budget requirements. They help in estimating the cost of any proposed project. They show up also the need to improve conditions.

Application of Performance Standards

For applying any staff formula or Performance

standards some basic information you will need: They relate to:

A. The number of working hours required in a year,

B. The number of work days expected of a person,

C. The productive work hours per person (i.e. **B** minus frictional loss).

D. The frictional loss is about 25%.

Let us assume that:

A is 3,120 hours (=10 hours per day x 6 days a week x 52weeks in a year).

B is 210 days (= 365 days minus eligible holidays and leave days, i.e. 22 holidays + 52 Sundays +12 Second Saturdays + 20 Casual Leave + 33 Earned Leave + 16.5 Half Pay Leave).

C is 4.5 hours (= 6 hours of work per day minus 25% frictional loss).

Therefore, if we divide the figure showing the total work load arrived at in the case of each specific **function, activity, work** or **job** in terms of man hours by 4.5 (the productive work hours) we can arrive at the total **number of man days** required to complete that function, activity, work or job as the case may be; and then if we divide the total number of man days required for running a library as a whole, or an activity or function thereof, we will know the total staff strength needed in an year.

QUALIFICATIONS OF STAFF

After having estimated the workload and the manpower requirement generally, jobs identified should be categorized into 'Professional' and 'Non-professional'; then the different levels of staff required in each category is decided upon; and finally the numbers in each category and level should be estimated. Five possible positions are there in a library / information centre:

1. Head,

2. Senior Professionals,
3. Senior Information Analysts,
4. Junior Information Analysts, and
5. Information Assistants.

Not all of them need the same qualifications. **Knowledge, skill, and attitude** are the threefold requirement of library staff.

Knowledge

Knowledge may be subject knowledge and/or professional knowledge. Persons with the traditional library education may not fit well in all places of a modern library/ information centre. A combination of professional training and subject specialization is what is desirable. Qualifications required for each specific service can be different. For example, knowledge required on the part of Senior Professionals to manage information consolidation services and products can be the sum total or a good mix of all the following:

- Methods for studying new subjects;
- Data/information analysis techniques;
- Methods for conducting user studies;
- Methods for identifying and selecting core documents /journals;
- Knowledge of different types of information consolidation services/products and their preparation;
- Techniques for directory preparation;
- Techniques for evaluation of information products/ services;
- Techniques for consolidation and integration including packaging and repackaging of information;
- Techniques of technical writing;
- Techniques of Information presentation;

- Techniques of preparation of various audiovisual aids.

Skills

Skills necessary can be listed as follows:

- Traditional skills of acquiring and organizing and disseminating information;
- Skills in communication systems analysis, interpersonal relationship, financial planning, marketing , etc,
- Managerial skills in technology management, problem solving, and decision making;
- Skills to analyze, synthesize, interpret, consolidate and evaluate Information and knowledge;
- Skills to interact with users and recognize their information needs;
- Skills to organize and manage a team of staff for the preparation of various information products and services;
- Skills to identify the products to be prepared for different user groups;
- Skills to identify and select the relevant information;
- Skills to process and evaluate the information;
- Skills to consolidate and integrate the information into an organized text.

Attitude

Despite good qualifications and many skills what might spoil the name of a library is the absence of the right attitude in library staff. Librarianship is not just a dignified occupation but it is a noble service. The selfless, sacrificing attitude is very much typical of library personnel. They must be inviting and willing to volunteer hardships for satisfying their clients without anticipating any personal benefits whatsoever. At the same time they must make the client go back with the feeling that whatever care and services they received were **not just**

gifts but their rights only. Library staff should not scare away readers but on the other hand after every service episode the client must go back convinced that the library is worth coming back. Repeated visits are always reckoned as testimonies of user satisfaction. On the other hand, however qualified and skilled may be a particular staff, without proper attitude and other personal qualities the person will be a professional failure in a library.

Competencies as Information Professionals

Generally, two sets of competencies are required for information professionals, i.e. ***Professional competencies*** and ***Personal competencies***. The former are related to practitioner's knowledge of information sources, access, technology and management. They involve specific skills in managing the information organization, the information resources, the information services, and the application of information tools and technologies. Personal competencies, on the other hand, represent a set of attitudes, skills and values that enable practitioners to work effectively and contribute positively to their organization, clients and profession. These competencies range from being strong communicators, to demonstrating the value-add of their contributions while remaining flexible and positive in an ever changing environment. There are also some *Core Competencies* which should anchor the professional and personal competencies. Two core competencies are absolutely essential for every information professional. They are the competencies in **understanding the value of developing and sharing their knowledge**, and in **adhering to the ethics of the profession**. Both professional and personal competencies should enable the practitioner to use this knowledge as a basis for providing the highest quality information services.

Competencies as Knowledge Managers

Along with the growth of the knowledge economy where knowledge is the economic driving factor, the recognition of knowledge as the driver of productivity and economic growth has led to a new focus on the role of information professionals. The term knowledge-based economy refers to the increased reliance on knowledge and innovation in the creation of products and services. In this paradigm shift from material goods to intangible knowledge goods, industrial libraries are recognizing a new and needy role of being **knowledge management centres**. This necessitates that information professionals should transform themselves into knowledge professionals or knowledge managers. The following chart will show the combination of various competencies required of the new generation of knowledge professionals (Al-Hawamdeh, 2003,p.178):

The competencies required of Knowledge Managers under the 6 categories of skills shown above, are identified and listed below:

1. Leadership and Management Skills:
   - In devising strategies
   - In motivating knowledge workers and encourage KM practices
   - In promoting knowledge sharing

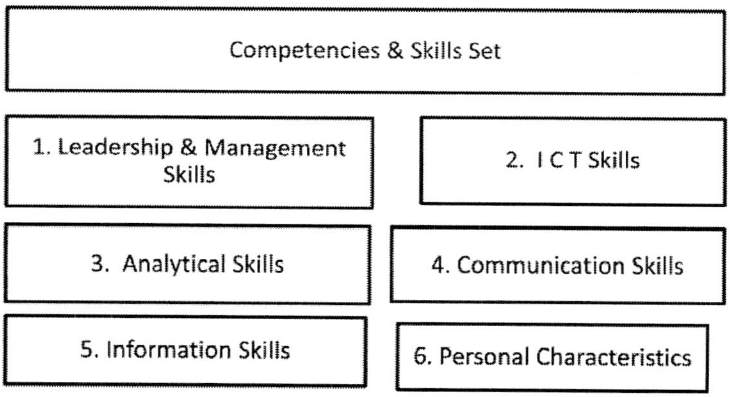

Fig. 8.2. Showing Competence Required of Knowledge Managers

- In managing internal and external knowledge resources
- In analyzing trends and providing directions

2. ICT Skills:
   - Familiarity with IT and KM tools
   - Good knowledge of in-house KM tools
   - Good knowledge of emerging technologies and likely impact on the organization
3. Analytical Skills:
   - In understanding business process
   - In exhibiting and promoting system thinking
   - In visualizing complex environment
   - In thinking logically
   - In relating to the organizational business objectives
4. Communication Skills:
   - In interacting with knowledge workers and management
   - In communicating clearly in oral and written form
   - In persuading and convincing
   - In being a good listener and connector
5. Information Skills:
   - In information seeking and needs assessing
   - In information acquisiton
   - In information organization
   - In information evaluation and filtering
   - In information sysnthesis
   - In information packaging
   - In information visualiztion
6. Personal Characteristics:
   - Proactive and responsive

- Creative and innovative
- Friendly and sensitive
- Self-confident and pleasant personality
- Patient and flexible
- Diverse subject background

HUMAN RESOURCES DEVELOPMENT (HRD)

One must understand that in modern management science there has been a conceptual shift from Personnel Management (PM) to Human Resources Management (HRM). PM was a traditional and reactive approach to problems of staff management when staff was viewed as an organization's biggest expense and a mere means to an end, and staff development was a way of solving problems. HRM, in contrast, views staff as the organization's greatest asset and accordingly sees staff training and development as due investment in that asset. Human Resources Development (HRD) is the part of HRM that specifically deals with training and development of all employees. HRD begins with training an individual after he/she is first hired, by providing opportunities to learn new skills, distributing resources that are beneficial to the employee's tastes, and any other developmental activities. HRD has been defined by experts as *"a set of systematic and planned activities designed by an organization to provide its members with the opportunities to learn necessary skills to meet current and future demands"* (Werner & De Simone, 2006). HRD has been an important topic of study and research in current management literature. While management professionals generally consider HRD as a sub-discipline of HRM, some researchers have broadened its scope by looking at it from socio-economic angle and giving it other dimensions such as physical, intellectual, psychological, social, political, moral and spiritual development of individuals and groups.

HRD in Libraries

Now, coming to the context of Science Library management with which we are directly concerned, HRD has a special significance as libraries and information centres are predominantly service providers where user satisfaction is very much impacted by quality of services rendered which in turn is governed by staff competency. Therefore, while planning the 'Personnel Requirements' of the Science Information System there must be proper provision given for the HRD component also. The focus of all aspects of HRD is on developing the most superior workforce so that the entire library, and every individual employee thereof, can accomplish the work goals in the service to its customers. The HRD framework should help employees to develop their personal and organizational skills, knowledge, and abilities. HRD activities may range from employee training, career development, performance management and development, coaching, mentoring, success planning, and key employee identification to organizational development. They can be informal such as when an employee being coached by a senior staff at joining duty, learning at workplace as on-the-job training, or can be formal such as in class room training; by sending staff for relevant course programmes, workshops, seminars or conferences; by participating in trainings imparted by software dealers or database vendors, casual instructions in installing special software packages or in tackling simple hardware or software problems, etc.

Identifying Training Needs

Systematic HRD efforts should begin with trying to understand the training needs of individuals and groups of staff. Surveys can be made of the whole staff to discover the training needs which staff feel they have. Further, there can be organizational training needs which relate to the general weaknesses in the library which can be remedied by training.

The weaknesses have to be assessed in relation to the present and future objectives of the organization. Training needs can also be identified through a scrutiny of jobs being poorly performed in the library, so to say in terms of quantitative and qualitative standards.

Staff appraisal can be a valuable aid in identifying individual training needs. Deficiencies can be noted as categorized as weaknesses in knowledge, skills and attitude. It is advisable to have a regular staff review procedure with at least three objectives:

(a) recognition of the contributions made by individuals,

(b) further assistance needed for individuals to develop their full potential as quickly as possible, and

(c) assistance needed for the institution to make the most effective use of its staff.

The introduction of an appraisal system directed towards developing staff potential, assisting in the improvement of performance, and enhancing career and promotion opportunities, and thereby improving performance of the institution as a whole, is very much desirable. Always prefer a staff appraisal scheme with firm structures and frame works. Here there are two steps, viz. self-appraisal, and performance review.

For self-appraisal it is good to use a well designed preparatory **self-appraisal form** to serve as the basis for an **appraisal interview**. This can be a self administering questionnaire to be got filled up by individual staff members which can contain data fields to suggest their strengths, weaknesses, and training needs. The real benefit of staff appraisal lies in regular and effective follow-up of an agreed action plan, like **performance reviews**. A different set of questionnaire can be got filled up by the reviewers or supervisory staff. All categories of staff should be covered by such review and appraisal system, may be professional seniors, professional juniors, non-professionals, clerical, or manual staff. The reviewers have to use any standard appraisal form like the ALA Standard Rating Form.

Staff Motivation

Motivating staff is the most important aspect of Personnel Management or Human Resources Management. But, **how to motivate the library staff?** Some may say, by promoting their job satisfaction, or by creating in them the feeling of being valued by others, or by giving opportunities for self-fulfillment. But in practice these may be not that easy, because, not everyone is motivated in the same way. Staff development programmes, and development of team spirit are other possible ways.

HRD programmes for LIS personnel are many and varied. Many fall in the category of continuing education also. Generally, they can be grouped under four heads:

- Library training events,
- On-the-Job development,
- Professional activities, and
- Self-paced learning.

Library training events can include:

- Staff induction/ orientation programmes/In-service training,
- Lectures or talks by experts,
- Short courses,
- In-house conferences, seminars or workshops; and
- Periodical staff meetings / training hours.

On-the-Job development may include:

- Job rotation,
- Shadowing,
- Project work,

- Quality circles,
- Delegation to new jobs, .

Professional activities may be:

- Membership networks,
- Outside conferences, seminars, workshops
- Exhibitions, Book fairs, etc.
- Professional get-togethers / meetings.

Self –paced Learning includes:

- Guided reading of LIS literature
- Visiting other libraries
- Informal discussions with colleagues
- Interactive media,
- Distance learning for formal qualifications, etc.

CONCLUSION

In conclusion, we must know that "*Manpower Planning can be defined as a strategy for the acquisition, utilization, improvement and retention of an enterprise's human resources*". In all enterprises, including a library or information centre, the personnel will be encountering many problems. In solving these problems, first of all, their motivations have to be understood and morale has to be promoted. Their salary / pay structure, job security, promotion / advancement, control and supervision, working conditions, inter-personal relations, recognition / status, etc. are matters affecting their performance. The following general guidelines may be borne in mind:

- Systematic selection and recruitment of staff;
- Appropriate placement of individual staff;
- Adequate training and orientation for all;
- Systematic management principles:

- Pay and other benefits commensurate with qualifications and competence;
- Appreciation and recognition of talents / achievements;
- Providing conducive work environment.

REFERENCES

AL-HAWAMDEH, Suliman,(2003), *Knowledge management; cultivating knowledge professionals*, Oxford, Chandos Publishing, 2003.

CORRALL, Sheila and BREWERTON, Antony (1999), *The new professional's handbook; your guide to information services.* London, Library Association, 1999.

CORRALL, Sheila (2000), *Strategic management of information services; a planning handbook*, Taylor & Francis, 2005 (2000).

DHIMAN, Anil K and RANI, Yashoda (2005),, *Learn Library management*, (New Delhi, Ess. Ess. Publns, 2005.

"Human Resources Management (HRM): Definition and Concept" *www.managementstudyguide.com* Retrieved on 26-08-2020)

JORDAN, Peter and JONES, Noragh (1987), *Staff management in library and information work*, edn. 3. England, Gower Publishing Company, 1987.

Oxford Languages / Google's English Dictionary

RANGANATHAN, S.R. (1959), *Library Administratio*, edn 2, Bombay, Asia Publishing House, 1959.

SEETHARAMA, S. (1990), *Guidelines for planning of libraries and information centres*, Calcutta, IASLIC, 1990.

WERNER, John M. and DE SIMONE (2012) *Human Resources Development* Edn.6, South Western Cengage Learning, Mason, OH USA.

9
Financial Planning and Budgeting

Estimating financial requirements or budgeting of a library or information centre is a very serious task. This is in fact the sum total of our studies related to the other aspects, like user requirements, information sources available, collection development, technical organization, information services to be provided, and personnel requirements. There are at least four questions to be examined here:

1. How to know and estimate the financial requirements of an information centre?
2. How to secure the finances?
3. How to regulate the income and expenditure?
4. How to justify the expenditure?

These are the problems confronting librarians / information centre managers generally in planning and development of libraries or information centres.

BUDGETS & BUDGETARY METHODS

Budgeting as an activity has to be viewed as an essential occasion for estimating the financial requirements of a library, the availability of funds, and the allocation of the available funds. If so, you must necessarily know what is a Budget?

Budget is

(a) a financial plan of the estimated revenues and expenditures of an organization for a given period of time;

(b) a forecast of the means of carrying the plan into effect; and

(c) an indicator of the amount of money assigned to specific purposes.

There are different Budgetary Methods which we need to be familiar with. Some of these are explained below:

Item-Budgeting

This type of budget is also called 'Line Item Budget' or even 'Line by Line Budget'. Here various items of expenditure are listed successively and their corresponding figures are given, for example:

Salaries	-	Rs 10,00,000
Books and periodicals	-	7,00,000
Binding	-	1,00,000
Photocopying	-	1,00,000
Furniture & equipment	-	4,00,000
Contingencies	-	2,00,000
Total	=	**Rs 25,00,000**

This is the traditional budgetary method. This is relatively easy to prepare, present and understand. Usually prepared by marginal enhancements over previous year's budget it does not involve any review of the provisions in the previous budgets and their utilization. One advantage is that it ensures that the funds budgeted will be spent. The budget is inflexible because financial rules would not permit shifting of expenditures from one head to another.

Programme Budgeting

This is a relatively new concept in budgeting for libraries. Here the proposed expenses are categorized by functions to be undertaken and accomplished. It is a "what purpose budget". It will have a direct bearing on the library operations and services as the funds allocated will reveal. For example, the budget will list proposed estimates or allocations under heads, like

Documentation work	=	Rs 100,000
Publishing work,	=	50,000
Current Awareness Service	=	20,000
Library Orientation Programmes	=	30,000

The focus of this budgetary method is on the library's activities, and funds are earmarked for programmes or services that the library plans to provide. It is prepared not on the basis of unit cost of work, but on the basis of estimated total cost of individual programmes. Libraries normally have a functional organization and different departments or sections will be dealing with their own activities or programmes, such as acquisition, classification and cataloguing, reference and information services, documentation, etc. The programme budgeting method gives an opportunity for heads of various departments/ sections to gauge their requirements and ask for budget provisions. Continuity of programmes is optional every year.

Performance Budgeting or Unit Cost Budgeting.

Here unit costs are calculated for each item of work or activity. At first, the quantum of work is estimated and then the amount of money required is arrived at on the basis of unit costs, (i. e. unit costs x volume of work). For example,

Catalogue conversion work 100,000 records x Rs 5/-	= Rs 5,00,000
Digitalization of old books 100,000 pages x Rs7.50)	= Rs 7,50,000

Performance budgeting is almost similar to the Programme budgeting the only difference being the shift of emphasis from programmes to performance. The expenditure is based on the performance and therefore operational efficiency is of prime consideration. This requires careful collection of quantitative data on all the activities over a period of time. Management techniques, such as cost-benefit analysis, are used here to measure the performance and to establish norms. Thus, Performance Standards have great relevance in this budgetary method.

Planning – Programming - Budgeting System (PPBS)

PPBS is a much talked of budgeting method. Here the expenditures are analyzed in relation to their purpose. There will be a statement of objectives, an examination of the alternatives proposals to achieve each objective with their respective costs, and a final choice of the proposed programme. This method combines the best of both Programme Budgeting and Performance Budgeting. The focus in this method is on planning which begins with the establishment of goals and objectives, and ends with formulation of programmes or services. As in the case with Performance Budgeting the controlling aspect of measurement is central to PPBS.

Zero Based Budgeting (ZBB)

Conceptually this is similar to PPBS. The only difference is that ZBB does not take into account what happened in the past, but places emphasis on the currently proposed activities. Every programme or activity is spelled out in detail and the financial requirements are worked out without any reference to the past.

COMPONENTS OF A SCIENCE LIBRARY BUDGET

In this section, we will try to understand 'what are the financial requirements of the Science Library / Information Centre', or any library for that matter. This is in fact a cost analysis exercise. This has to be done based on types of costs incurring in a library / information centre. Costs can be separated into **'fixed costs'**, **'variable costs'**, **'direct costs'**, and, **'associated costs'**. The budgetary / financial requirements of a library / information centre are to be identified under three types of costs, viz.

(a) Initial costs / Start up costs,

(b) Annual Operating costs / Recurring expenses, and

(c) Future needs.

A library / information centre may propose or anticipate expenses under the following 6 heads:

1. Facilities,
2. Equipment & Furniture,
3. Salaries & wages,
4. Documents,
5. Materials & supplies / consumables, and
6. Miscellaneous.

We can now try to identify and list the items of expenditure that may occur under the three types of costs mentioned as (a), (b) and (c).

1. Facilities

(a) Initial costs : Physical plant of the library i.e. the construction of buildings, preparation of space by reconstruction, renovation, or new partitions, lighting, interior decoration, etc.

(b) Annual costs : annual repairs / reconditioning or maintenance as required.

(c) Future costs : Extensions, new facilities, face lifting, etc.

2. Equipment & Furniture

(a) Initial costs : Purchase of new items for the initial establishment.

(b) Annual costs : Repairs & maintenance of the existing items, purchase of additional items, AMC for computers & equipment, etc.

(c) Future costs : New equipment & furniture that will become necessary later.

3. Salaries & wages

(a) Initial costs : Consultancy costs, other non-recurring fees, charges, etc.

(b) Annual costs : Salaries of Professional & Non-professional, Clerical and menial staff.

(c) Future costs : Provision for periodical rises in salaries & wages, like pay revisions, cost of expansions / additions of staff and new appointments.

4. Documents

(a) Initial costs : Purchase of basic collection of books, journals and secondary publications, and other information sources.

(b) Annual Costs : Additions to collections, Subscriptions to journals, databases, license fees, etc.

(c) Future costs : Cost of probable extensions of collections to new subject areas/ specialties.

5. Materials & Supplies / Consumables

(a) Initial costs : Initial supplies of printing, stationery, etc.

(b) Annual costs : Replenishing the stock of all expendables.

(c) Future costs : Contingencies.

6. Miscellaneous Costs

(a) Initial costs : expenses of planning and setting up.

(b) Annual costs : costs of travelling, running costs of motor vehicles, conveyance of staff, staff training, etc.

(c) Future costs : Evaluation costs at the close of a period, etc.

All the above items of expenses can be further classified and presented under three categories: **Capital costs, Other non-recurring costs**, and **Recurring Costs**.

BUDGET ALLOCATION

What should be the basis for Budget Allocation for a library or information centre as a whole? The only basis should be the needs of the library for the coming year and the cost of filling those needs at current market rates. How much finance needs to be provided will depend upon the quantity and quality of documents, the number and category of users, and the other factors relating to that particular library. There are some methods that could be generally employed in estimating the annual financial allocation for a library / information centre. They can be: (a) Per capital method (b) Method of details, and (c) Method of proportion.

Per capita method is supposed to be a more realistic and equitable approach to the library's annual financial needs. A minimum amount per head of population in each type or category of users might be recommended by organizations or bodies of authorities, like: Rs 20/- per student and Rs 300- per teacher as prescribed by Dr. Ranganathan for university and college libraries. But such recommendations are subject to change in view of changing costs and environments.

Method of details : This is the item-wise proposal in the budget based on the estimated needs, like Salaries, Books/ documents, Binding, Contingencies, etc. Every item in the budget might have been approached on different basis. For example, Cost of staff might be worked out on the basis of work load assessment and Staff Formula, while Cost of books & other reading materials might be estimated by using per capita method.

Method of proportion : This may sound to be an arbitrary principle. Nevertheless it has gained much acceptance. In this method, a certain minimum proportion or percentage of the total budget of the organization should be allocated for its library. For example, the IASLIC has recommended 2% of the total sales turn over in an industrial establishment, and 6.25% of the research budget in a research institution, for their libraries. These proportions need timely changes as situations demand.

MODEL LIBRARY BUDGET

Given below is a model budget for a Science Library with all essential details. This may be taken only as a general guideline for preparing and presenting the budget. Also see the explanations given after the model.

MODEL ANNUAL BUDGET FOR A SCIENCE LIBRARY

A. Capital costs

1. Additional Space for I T Section
   Including cabin creation and interior
   decoration Lump sum provision = Rs 6,00,000
2. Purchase of new computers,
   equipment & accessories = Rs 12,00,000

   Total = Rs 18,00,000

B. Recurring Costs

1. SALARIES

   Chief Librarian (1)
   (Rs. 37,400 – 67,000) + DA 17% = 168,714 × 12
   = Rs. 20,24,568

   Assistant Librarians/ Professional Assistants (2)
   (Rs 15,600 – 39,100) + DA 17% = 93,366 × 2 × 12
   = Rs.22,40,784

Assistant Librarians/ Professional Assistants (2)
(Rs 15,600 – 39,100) + DA 17% = 67,509 × 2 × 12
= Rs 16,20,216

Non-professional Assistants (4)
(Rs. 9,300 – 34,800) + DA 17% = 62,127 × 4 × 12
= Rs. 29,82,096

Peons/watchmen (4)
(Rs.5,200 – 20,200) +DA 17% =29,835 × 4 × 12
= Rs.14,32,080

Total **= Rs.1,02,99,744**

Rounded off to = Rs.1,03,00,000

2. DOCUMENTS

Books (lump sum provision) = Rs 30,00,000

Journals & Newspapers (lump sum provision)
= Rs 20,00,000

Electronic resources (at INDEST-AICTE Consortia prices) = Rs 30,00,000

Total **= Rs 80,00,000**

3. PROJECTS, PROGRAMMING & SERVICES

Catalogue conversion = Rs 10,00,000

Digitization of old books = Rs. 10,00,000

CAS and SDI services = Rs. 5,00,000

Information marketing = Rs. 5,00,000

HRD Programmes = Rs. 5,00,000

Seminars & Workshops = Rs. 5,00,000

Total **= Rs 40,00,000**

4. CONTINGENCIES

Light, power & water = Rs 4,80,000

Printing & Stationery = Rs 5,00,000

Postage & Courier = Rs 2,00,000

Telephone & Internet	= Rs 7,20,000
Cleaning & upkeep	= Rs 4,00,000
Travel & conveyance	= Rs 10,00,000
AMC for computers & equipment	= Rs 2,00,000
Total	**= Rs 35,00,000**
5. OTHER UNFORESEEN EXPENSES:	
Lump sum provision	**= Rs 4,00,000**
Grand Total of A & B	**Rs. 2,80,00,000**

Allocation of Funds

Allocation of funds within the total library budget may vary from place to place. In developed countries, a 50 - 60% on Staff salary, and the remaining for Documents and all expenses together may be a usual practice. In India norms are only evolving. Dhiman & Rani, (2005) have suggested 50% for Staff, 35% for Documents, 9% for Equipment, and 6% for all the rest. These suggestions would appear too unrealistic to Indian conditions. In view of the rising cost of books and journals this has to be in the reverse order, say 40 - 50 % for Documents and the rest for all other expenses including Staff salary. The increasing importance of electronic resources and the rising cost of electronic databases warrant the budgets of a special library to be drastically re-adjusted. The INDEST-AICTE consortia, for example, expects its member libraries to pay a total of Rs. 1.40 crores towards the price of 16 e-resources they are covering now (as per their 2013 price list). The model budget given here has provided only Rs 30 lakhs for some chosen items from the consortium list.

The allocations made in the model budget do not conform to any recommendation whatsoever but is based on practical needs, which is as follows:

Capital costs	= Rs. 18 lakhs (6.43%).
Documents including e-resources	= Rs. 80 lakhs (28.57%).

Staff salary	= Rs. 103 lakhs (36.78%).
Programmes / Services	= Rs. 40 lakhs (14.28%).
Contingencies & Other expenses	= Rs. 39 lakhs (13.94%
Total	**= Rs. 280 lakhs (100%).**

Presentation of the Budget

Many things about estimating the cost of establishing and running a science library and preparing its budget have been discussed already. The budget should be not only carefully and systematically prepared but also it should be properly presented to the authorities for approval. The budget document is an official document to be circulated among and seen by several administrative and financial officials of the parent organization. Hence, it should be self-contained with regard to the activities and services of the library, self-explanatory, well organized and neatly presented. Every item of expenditure and its proposed allocation need to be discussed with references to its past allocations, if any. The budget document, besides the relevant statements, tables, figures, etc. forming its body, must have an **Explanatory Memorandum** or an Executive Summary. It should discuss the goals and objectives of the library in brief, activities and accomplishments of the previous year, anticipated activities and proposed targets for the budgeted year, and the future perspectives. The officials who are responsible for providing funds will quite naturally want to know why the funds are required. Please remember that there will be several other claimants for the available funds. Hence, they will consider critically the merits of library's request in relation to those of other departments and the total financial resources at their disposal. Hence, our claims should be justified and demands convincing.

REFERENCES

AL-HAWAMDEH, Suliman (2003), *Knowledge management; cultivating knowledge professionals*, Oxford, Chandos Publishing, 2003.

CORRALL, Sheila and BREWERTON, Antony (1999), *The new professional's handbook; your guide to information services*. London, Library Association, 1999.

CORRALL, Sheila (2005), *Strategic management of information services; a planning handbook*, Taylor & Francis, 2005 (2000).

HIMAN, Anil K and RANI, Yashoda (2005), *Learn Library management*, (New Delhi, Ess. Ess. Publns, 2005.

JORDAN, Peter and JONES), Noragh (1987), *Staff management in library and information work*, edn. 3. England, Gower Publishing Company, 1987.

RANGANATHAN, S.R. (1959), *Library Administration*, edn 2, Bombay, Asia Publishing House, 1959.

SEETHARAMA, S. (1990), *Guidelines for planning of libraries and information centres*, Calcutta, IASLIC, 1990.

10
Evaluation of Library and Information Systems

In the earlier chapters of the book we have dealt with the planning and developing of science libraries and information centres/systems, and the different facets of that subject. In this final chapter we are going to see how a library or information centre can be evaluated. Evaluation is a continuous activity in the planning and development process of any information system. In fact, planning leads to designing, and evaluation leads to re-designing. Systems are thus being continuously kept upgraded or improved upon. Library as a system is no exception to this general rule. There are different methods in evaluation (Bavakutty &.Abdul Majeed , 2005). But library being a service organization it is best evaluated based on its performance. Therefore, in this chapter, we will give necessary exposure to a major method of library evaluation, namely Performance Measurement with an account of Cost-Benefit Analysis. Further, there are in this chapter some sections that deal with some new management tools for evaluating and measuring the quality and efficiency of services in libraries. These are the SERVQUAL, the LibQUAL, and the SWOT Analysis, and we will explain how these techniques could be applied in evaluating any library or information system.

STATISTICAL REPORTING

Traditionally libraries have been evaluated on the basis of statistical reporting, like how many members it served, how many visited the library, how many volumes were added to the stock, how many books were issued for home reading, etc. Such statistical reporting is only a simple quantification method without any attempt at analysis (*OECD Glossary of Statistical Terms*). There is difference between evaluation based on 'how good a library is' and 'how much good a library does'. For many years librarians have been justifying their libraries through the statistics in Annual Reports. Only when the figures in the statistical reporting increase over years they are to be seen as an indication of growth. But the defect of these indicators of growth is that they are not correlated to the needs and demands made upon the library – firstly, to assess the efficiency / effectiveness of the activities provided, or secondly to know whether they are the right activities and in proper balance. This is not done because libraries are often taken for granted as a good thing, and does not need any special justification.

PERFORMANCE MEASUREMENT (PM)

The conviction that a library or information centre must be evaluated based on its performance has led to the application of an well established evaluation method called 'Performance Measurement' (PM) which allows evaluation based on qualitative terms. PM is a management tool designed to assist managers to determine how well an organization or any of its services is performing. It **provides evidences to base judgments**, although they are not judgments in themselves (Abbot, 1994). PM is not an exact science, but it helps us in making comparative judgments with precise calculations and meticulous data. Hence, PM can be used to assess libraries and information centres according to the good they do – the effectiveness, the cost-effectiveness, and the efficiency of their services. PM can describe the activities of a library by using some criteria called 'Performance Indicators'.

Origin and Development of PM

PM has been there in Library and Information services since the late 1960s (Boekhorst,1995). During these 50 years, a wealth of literature has been made available on this subject. They range from highly theoretical to the detailed and practical. Some involve mathematical concepts and statistical methods. Published items are more on identifying Performance Indicators rather than on their implementation. However, there is wide spread acceptance of the need of PM, although their systematic application or implementation are too poor. This may be because:

1. librarians generally do not have the requisite skills to undertake PM. Hence, there has been no progress beyond theory.
2. there is pressure of time and need to maintain services on day to day basis; and
3. the difficulties involved in developing Performance Indicators.

Why then this persisting interest in performance measurement as a subject of study? This again may be due to:

1. the pressure from outside the library or parent institution; and
2. the most enduring argument that PM is an essential part of good management.

Developing performance indicators is an integral part of the management process.

Need for PM in Libraries

There are different reasons why PM is forced upon libraries / information centres:

1. Economic Need : Libraries have to function today in a harsher economic climate where competition for resources allocation is fierce. Therefore, libraries must demonstrate their value in measurable ways.

2. Political imperatives : National political imperatives encourage greater efficiency and accountability in public services. Such pressures have even led to the imposition of a set of Performance Indicators as are prescribed by some concerned bodies, like the UGC or AICTE.

3. Accountability to the Parent Institution : Since there will be competitive demands for resource allocation from different departments, librarians have to justify the resources they consume and demonstrate before the authorities who grant the funds that the benefits derived to the user community are worth the expenditure. Describing the range, extent and importance of the services they provide they must convince their political masters and all others concerned that they are not wasting resources, instead "they offer not just value, but value for money".

4. Accountability to the customers : Customer rights are now becoming more and more prevalent in many areas of services. In library and information services also this will become enforceable, if not already now, and librarians will have to be accountable to their users.

5. For facilitating grounds for service agreements in services : In situations where library and information services are provided on contractual basis for the benefit of an outside organization, it is necessary to frame meaningful and quantifiable agreements and to monitor their compliances. Performance indicators will serve this purpose.

6. For Quality Management : Performance indicators have value and relevance in quality management and quality assurance. They enable measurement of the quality achievements (Verma..2002).

7. For Decision Support : Performance indicators are important tools for library managers in decision making areas such as resources allocation, priority setting, and planning for future activities.

Advantages /Uses of PM

We may now know about the specific uses or advantages of PM to library managers:

- to understand what the library is achieving;
- to monitor the library's progress year on year, and in comparison with other libraries and projects;
- to gauge how efficiently and effectively library operations and services are performing;
- to take decisions about future resourcing of service areas on the basis of information on past performance;
- to estimate the consequences of past increase or decrease in resources for different services;
- to check whether the objectives of the library as a whole are accurately reflected in the balanced activities of the library or not.

Statistics Vs. Indicators

'Statistics' are only simple quantification of activities, like the number of book issues, the number of registered borrowers, the total number of visits to the library, etc. These are important figures which provide some insight into the size and scope of a library's operations, but they do not facilitate any quality judgment of the library's services. On the other hand, Performance Indicator also can be used as a quantitative expression of the use or value of any aspect of library service. Such indicators are normally derived by combining two statistics to form a ratio. For example, the number of book loans can be divided by the number of registered library users to produce a ratio, i.e. average loans per registered borrower. This can be seen as an effectiveness indicator of the library. Statistics does not tell anything about the library's performance. Annual reports give statistics. But there the emphasis is on description and not on analysis. In some cases comparative year–on-statistics will give us performance information. For example, library issues rose by 5% on the previous year. This figure if taken in isolation does not demonstrate any improvement in performance. It could illustrate increased effectiveness of service if the user population had remained the same or decreased from previous year. The difference in registered library borrowers, the length of loan period, etc. will affect the results.

Performance Indicators

In PM, it' is possible to visualize the following conceptual model of a library.

INPUTS → OUTPUTS → OUTCOMES

The different elements in this model can be defined as follows:

(A) INPUTS : Resources inputted like Staff, Materials, Capital fund, etc.

(B) OUTPUTS : The direct products of the library's operations, like loans transacted, enquiries answered, materials catalogued, exhibitions held, seminars conducted, etc..

(C) OUTCOMES : Uses made by the consumer of a given output and the degree of satisfaction obtained from those outputs.

(D) ENVIRONMENTAL STATISTICS : Inputs, Outputs, and Outcomes are to some extent within the control of the library or of its funding body. There are other data elements beyond the control of the library. These include basic statistics about the user population, locality, and environment. These are constraints on the library's operation and hence important information to be reckoned with in the choice or application of Performance Indicators. These are called Environmental Statistics, Examples are:

- population size (of potential users),
- registered users;

- geographical distribution of population;
- geographical distribution of users;
- population characteristics;
- user characteristics.

'Population' means the total number of potential users of the library.

'Registered users' - There is difference between registered users and active users. The former is to be taken from records, and the latter to be found from surveys.

'Geographic distribution' is of most importance in a public library system/network with branches. It is also important in educational libraries with split sites. In large companies with multi-sites or wide spread area 'geographic distribution' is very much relevant.

'Population characteristics' will include: age, sex, social class, occupation (for public libraries) status (student or staff in academic libraries), subject/ department of study, etc. (for educational libraries), and job type, site or area of work in the case of company libraries.

(E) HIGHER ORDER EFFECTS : They are beyond 'Outcomes" noted above. For example, the extent to which the services of the library affect the community served. Here evaluation is based on "Impact Indicators" For example, if a university library wishes to assess the impact of introducing a particular service, it must study the correlation between use made of that service and the instances of academic achievements (degree passed with I class or distinction). In the case of industrial library utilization the impact factor can be studied by correlating a particular service with a scientist's publications or research output.

But one difficulty or limitation in assessing the 'Higher Order Effects' of libraries by means of impact indicators is that there are a number of factors outside the library's control which determine whether a student will gain a first class / distinction or not, and whether a scientist will qualify for an award through the services of his institutional library. Consequently, Impact Indicators are difficult to interpret and act upon.

Generating Performance Indicators

The different elements in the conceptual model, viz. **inputs, Outputs, Outcomes, Environmental statistics,** and **Higher order effects**, operate in certain relationship to each other and can be compared in different ways. It is the relationship between the different elements that forms the focus for PM. (Appleton, 2017) The relationships can be defined as ***Economy, Market Penetration, Efficiency, Effectiveness, Cost-effectiveness,*** and ***Costs***. As mentioned earlier, the different elements in the conceptual model of the library operate in different relationships to each other and can be compared in different ways, like:

(a) Outputs & Inputs,

(b) Inputs & Environmental statistics,

(c) Outputs & Environmental Statistics,

(d) Outcome & Outputs,

(e) Inputs and & Outcomes

(a) Library Outputs & Inputs: The relationship between these two elements provides two types of indicators: (i) 'Efficiency Indicators', and (ii) 'Operational Indicators'.

Efficiency Indicators : With these, one can assess how efficiently an operation is carried out, from the customer's point of view. Hence, Efficiency Indicators can be expressed in terms of the Speed of Supply of a service. e.g. the through-put time for processes such as acquisition and cataloguing, or delivery time for inter-library loans, or time taken in answering of telephone reference enquiries, etc.

Operational Performance Indicators: The relationship between Outputs and Inputs can be used to generate information on the productivity of different services, and on costs of services. They can be grouped together as operational performance indicators and can be applied at service level of activities. For example, average number of transactions (such as loans transacted, enquiries answered, or online searches conducted) per relevant member of LIS staff; or unit cost of a transacted activity such as cost per enquiry answered, or cost per new catalogue record created.

(b) Library Inputs & Environmental Statistics : The relationship between these elements can generate indicators for knowing how economical a library is: For example: (i) Library expenditure per head of population /student / member of staff; (ii) Proportion of budget consumed by a given service. The 'indicators of economy' is used in isolation will not give insight into how well the library is performing (efficiency or effectiveness). They need be studied in comparison with different sites of the library system.

(c) Library Outputs & Environmental Statistics : These two elements in mutual relationship provide 'indicators of market penetration'. These can be applied at macro level / whole library service, for example: (i) Number of registered users as a percentage of the total population; (ii) Degree of correlation between population characteristics and user characteristics (to find out under-represented groups and to investigate reasons for this). 'Market Penetration indicators' can be also applied to the take-up of specific services, for example: (i) Percentage of potential market who make use of a Current Awareness Service, (ii) Percentage of scientist population in the company attending the User Education Programme.

(d) Outcomes & Outputs : By relating Outcomes to Outputs 'Effectiveness Indicators' can be generated. Some of these can be indirect measures, like the turnover rate of stock, and the accuracy and timeliness of supply of product or service (promptness). However, the best measure of the effectiveness of a service must be the actual satisfaction which users feel with that service. Therefore, direct feedback from readers is necessary for the majority of effectiveness indicators. The most used indicators of user satisfaction involve measures of either failure or need-fill rate. Failure rate assesses the extent to which customers fail to find what they want. Need-fill rate studies the extent to which customers' expressed needs (demands) are met by library services.

(e) Inputs & Outcomes: By relating Inputs to Outcomes, 'Cost-effectiveness Indicators' can be derived. They compare the effectiveness achieved in providing a given level of service with the cost of achieving that level; or the cost of providing a service with the number of active users (the degree of 'market penetration') of that service.

Examples of Performance Indicators

The following table gives some examples for measuring the various operations and activities of a library / information centre:

	Activity	*Indicator*	*Basis of measure*
1.	Acquisition	• Efficiency • Effectiveness • Costs • Productivity	• Speed of supply. • Accuracy of supply. • Unit cost of supply. • Items processed per relevant member of staff.
2.	Cataloguing & Classification	• Efficiency • Effectiveness • Cost-effectiveness • Costs • Productivity	• Delay time/through put. • Accuracy of services. • Timeliness of supply. • User failure rate at the Catalogue /Shelf. • Cost of different levels of cataloguing (compared with User failure rates at the Catalogue/shelf). • Unit cost of cataloguing and classification.

		• Items catalogued / classified per relevant number of staff.
3. Mediated Online Searching	• Economy	• Proportion of budget committed.
	• Market penetration	• Actual users as proportion of potential users.
	• Efficiency	• Time taken per search.
	• Effectiveness	• Surveys of needs fill rate.
	• Cost-effectiveness	• Costs per user (compared with the extent of market penetration/staff.
	• Costs	• Unit cost per search.
	• Productivity	• Number of searches conducted per relevant member of staff.
4. Current Awareness/ SDI service	• Market penetration	• Subscribers as proportion of potential subscribers.
	• Effectiveness	
	• Cost-effectiveness	• Surveys of need fill rate (User Satisfaction).
	• Costs	• Percentage of Repeat use.
	• Productivity	• Cost of service per subscriber of different standards of production.
		• Cost per bulletin produced/SDI service given.
		• Bulletins produced per relevant member of staff.

Fig. 10.1. Table showing Performance Indicators and their use in measuring Various Activities in a Library

We could see that different Performance Indicators can be identified out of the different combinations of data elements in the conceptual model of the library, namely, the Inputs, Outputs, Outcomes and Environmental statistics. In any Performance Assessment one indicator alone is rarely sufficient, but a range of indicators must be considered in combination.

Criteria for selection of Performance Indicators may include: Relevance/appropriateness, Helpfulness, Validity, Reliability, Practicability, etc. Objectivity in evaluation must be ensured at all costs, and that exactly is the purpose behind choice and application Performance Indicators (Abbot, 1994).

COST- BENEFIT ANALYSIS

This is one of the tools employed in Performance Evaluation based on the Cost-effectiveness Indicator. Particular projects or proposals can be compared to see whether the benefits outweigh the costs involved and therefore worthy of investment. The cost–benefit ratio itself can be used as a performance indicator to appraise or assess, the case of an existing product or service of the library, or a project proposal for a new one. Cost-benefit analysis is a type of economic evaluation that measures both costs and benefits, i.e. negative and positive consequences associated with a project proposal. It seeks to quantify all costs and benefits of a proposal in monetary terms, including even items which the market cost does not provide a satisfactory measure of economic value. As a technique, it can be used to compare the various costs associated with an investment with the benefits it might bring, over a number of years unto a future (Roberts, 1985).

There should be three sections in any cost-benefit analysis:

(A) Costs, (B) Benefits, and (C) Return on Investment.

(A) Costs : A detailed study of the various aspects of costs in budgeting has been given already in the previous chapter on 'Financial Planning and Budgeting'. Costs were examined there under six categories, viz.

1. Facilities
2. Equipment & Furniture,
3. Salaries & wages,
4. Documents,
5. Materials & supplies, and
6. Miscellaneous.

Each of these was seen under three subheads:

(i) Initial costs,
(ii) Annual costs, and
(iii) Future costs.

Costs occur in different areas, like: Capital costs, and Recurring costs. Capital costs include all money spent on purchase or lease of equipment, and their maintenance. There will be other capital costs like money spent on building and space provision, like in new constructions, or renovations of old buildings, or new partitioning and interior decorations, etc. Even, interest on the Capital Investments need be provided under Capital costs.

Recurring costs include expenditures involved for both Staff and Users. In the case of staff, their salary and all other emoluments as well as all overhead costs have to be accounted. On the part of Users, the value of time spent by them in obtaining the services have to be accounted for.

(B) Benefits : Benefits may be either Direct Benefits/ Savings, or (b) Measurable benefits, or (c) Intangible benefits.

(a) Direct benefits/savings are:
- costs that are reduced or eliminated by the service / system,
- like reduction in clerical personnel, or
- elimination of some specific costs like postage, stationery, etc., or

- reduction in costs due to improved procedures.

(b) Measurable benefits are:

- the money accruing to the institution through some features of the system / product / service, i.e. Cost gains through speed and accuracy.

(c) Intangible benefits are:

- certain advantages that are difficult to evaluate in terms of money. For example, better information leading to better decisions which in turn leading to greater efficiency. The 'Impact Factor" indicators in the Higher Order Effects can be used to assess these benefits.

(C) Return on Investments : Once costs and benefits are studied, the crucial part of the analysis is to know whether the system / product / service is worthwhile. Here, the pay-back time when the product brings back the money invested is to be assessed. The criterion is only financial (Roberts, 1985).

Thus, cost benefit analysis is a type of economic valuation in which both disadvantages (costs) and advantages (benefits) of an investment, purchase or process can be weighed and more financially viable decisions can be taken in a library or information centre.

SERVQUAL

As already mentioned in an earlier chapter there are some popular management tools that can be used for measuring service quality. Some researchers claim that SERVQUAL is the most popular assessment tool for service quality. It was designed by the Marketing Research Team consisting of Leonard L. Berry, A. Parasuraman and Valerea A. Zeithaml, in the 1980s, in the Texas A & M University (Parasuraman, 1991). Originally SERVQUAL employed 10 dimensions in the measurement of service quality, viz. Reliability, Responsiveness, Competence, Access, Courtesy, Communication, Credibility, Security, Understanding the customer, and Tangibles. But, in 1990s the authors refined the model by reducing to only 5 dimensions, viz. Reliability, Assurance, Tangibles, Empathy and Responsiveness. This new model began to be known by the acronym **RATER** representing the first letters of the 5 listed dimensions. This is a multiple-item scale used to measure customer expectations and perceptions of service quality (Coleman, Vicki, et al, 1997). RATER is a simple and useful model for qualitatively exploring and assessing customer's service experience and therefore began to be widely used by service delivery organizations. What SERVQUAL model does is discovering the gaps between users' perceptions and organization's expectations that should measure, manage and minimize. These are listed below:

Gap 1 is called '**Management Perception Gap'**. This is the difference between expected service by customers and the management's perceptions of the customers' expectations.

Gap 2 is called '**Quality Specification Gap'**. This is the difference between management's perception and the actual specification of the customer experience.

Gap 3 is called '**Service Delivery Gap'**. This is the difference between customer driven service design and standards of service delivery.

Gap 4 is called '**Market Communication Gap**'. This is the difference between the delivery of the customer experience and what is communicated to customers.

Gap 5 is called '**Perceived Service Quality Gap**'. This is the difference between customer's perceptions of the experience and the customer's expectation of the service.

As stated earlier, the efforts of the management should be to discover the gap between the customer's perceptions and expectations in the service provided and to initiate measures to minimize or bridge the available gap.

LibQUAL+

While SERVQUAL is assessment model useful for

business enterprises, LibQUAL is such a service quality measurement model developed particularly for measuring service quality in library and information centres. It had its origin in 1995 at the Texas A & M University when three of their professors, Zeithaml, Parasuraman and Berry started working with the SERVQUAL model for measuring service quality in the research libraries under the Association of Research Libraries (ARL) in USA and Canada. Having found SERVQUAL not fully suited to library service the team started developing an alternative protocol which they named LibQUAL+. In 2000, its pilot testing and evaluation were completed. LibQUAL+ includes the quantitative data relating to 22 core items and qualitative data provided by users in the form of open ended comments. The comments revealed the users' service quality perceptions as well as specific recommendations for quality improvement. By the year 2007 LibQUAL+ was being used in about 1,000 institutions from at least 17 countries and covered data from 1 million library users. The system supported then already 12 languages with a Chinese version being implemented in Hong Kong. Over a period of 8 years various editions of LibQual+ also have come out (Cook & Heath, 2001).

SWOT ANALYSIS

SWOT Analysis is a structured planning method used to evaluate the Strengths, Weaknesses, Opportunities and Threats involved in a project or in a business venture. This technique was evolved by Albert Humphrey at the Stanford Research Institute in the 1970s, using data taken from the Fortune 500 companies. It has become now one of the most renowned tools for the audit and analysis of the overall strategic position of a business and its environment (Humphrey, 2005). It is used as the foundation for evaluating the internal potential and limitations as well as the likely opportunities and threats from external environment. It uses under these four heads all positive and negative factors, both inside and outside of the firm that can affect its success. SWOT is an acronym for this management method, made from the first letters of the four factors: **S**trengths, **W**eaknesses, **O**pportunities and **T**hreats. Correct identification of the SWOTs is an important step in this exercise as only in that way it can help achieve the objective of the study. This technique is alternatively known as **SWOT Matrix** also. SWOT analysis helps in strategic planning in the following manner:

- It is a source of information for strategic planning;
- It helps to build up the organization's **strengths**;
- It reverses its **weaknesses**;
- It maximizes the response to **opportunities**;
- It helps to overcome the organization's **threats**;
- It can help in identifying the competencies of the organization; and
- It can help in setting of objectives for strategic planning.

The usefulness of SWOT analysis is not limited to profit making organizations. It can also be used in any decision making situation. These days we come across several SWOT analysis studies in the field of Library and Information Science also (Lali & Vijayakumar, 2002, Suresh, 2012). The Strength, Weaknesses, Opportunities and Threats of a given library as a whole, or a specific service or product of that library, can be subjected to SWOT analysis. The SWOT Analysis Matrix is presented in the chart below.

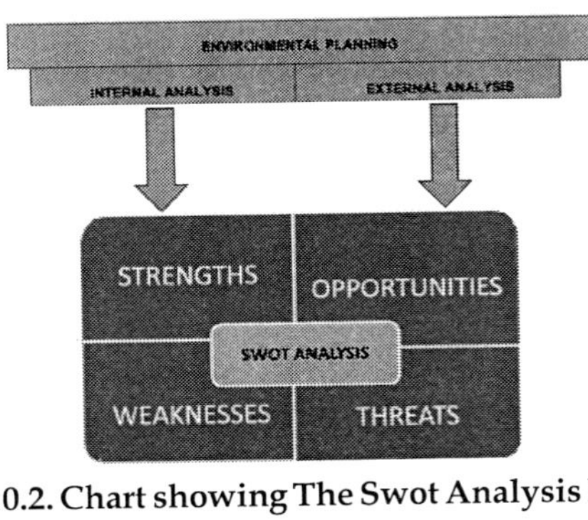

Fig. 10.2. Chart showing The Swot Analysis Matrix

STRENGTHS (Internal)	***WEAKNESSES (Internal)***	***OPPORTUNITIES (External)***	***THREATS (External)***
Collection; Equipment /ICT; Staff; Technical Organization; Information Services; Geographical position of the Library; Infrastructures; Furniture & facilities; Working days and Hours; Membership; Customer Care; Etc. etc.	Insufficient Investment; Inadequate Space; Lack of ICT infrastructure & equipment; Inadequate staff; Unqualified staff; Inadequate collection; Unsuited working days and hours; Etc. etc.	New Academic Programmes; New sources of funding; Co-operation & Consortia possibilities; New technologies; Etc. etc.	Other libraries in the neighborhood; Alternate information Providers; Changing Technologies/ ICT; Etc. etc.

Fig. 10.3. Table showing Possible Elements in the four SWOTS

The probable **elements in the four SWOTs** may be identified and listed as given in the above table. After having identified and listed them each element has to be assigned an appropriate value or score. The final position of the Matrix will reveal the balance or imbalance of the factors and the need if any for strategic planning for encountering the situation or for overcoming the Threats as well as exploiting the Opportunities.

CONCLUSION

This chapter has examined the subject of evaluation of libraries in much detail. We have come to realize that a library or information centre has to be evaluated mainly based on its performance, and that Performance Measurement is to be done based on suitable criteria called Performance Indicators, and that these indicators are being evolved out of the ratio between any two of the basic data elements relating to a library namely, Inputs, Outputs, Outcomes, Environmental Statistics and Higher Order Effects. We have also dealt with the practical use of these indicators for specific purposes with necessary guidelines regarding the choice and application of performance indicators. We have also discussed the technique of cost-benefit analysis as a tool in the economic evaluation of projects/products/services. In addition to both the above, we have covered some management tools, like SERVQUAL, LibQUAL and SWOT Analysis. And all the three have acquired a high degree of relevance and significance in current library management studies and in Library and Information Science research.

REFERENCES

ABBOTT, Christine (1994), *Performance measurement in library and information services*, London, ASLIB, 1994.

APPLETON (Leo) (2017), *Libraries and Key Performance Indicators: A Frame work for Practitioners*, Chandos Publishing, 2017.

ASIAN DEVELOPMENT BANK (2013), *Cost-Benefit Analysis for Development; A Practical Guide*, Institutional Document, January 2013.

BAVAKUTTY, M. & ABDUL MAJEED, K.C. (2005), *Methods of for measuring quality of libraries* New Delhi, Ess Ess Publns, 2005.

BOEKHORST, Peter te (1995), "Measuring Quality: the IFLA Guidelines for Performance Measurement in Academic Libraries" *IFLA Journal* Vol.21(4),1995, Pp.278-281.

COLEMAN, Vicki, et. al.(1997) "Toward a TQM paradigm: Using SERVQUAL to measure library service quality". *College and Research Libraries* Vol.58(3),1997.

COOK, C. & HEATH, F.(2001), "User's perceptions of library service quality: A LibQUAL qualitative study", *Library Trends Vol.* 49 (4), 2001,:pp.548-584.

GINES, de Rus (201o), *Introduction to Cost-Benefit Analysis: Looking for Reasonable Short Cuts*, Edward Edgar.

HUMPHREY, Albert (2005), "SWOT Analysis for Management Consulting" *SRI Alumni Newsletter*, Stanford Research Institute International.

LALI, S.L. and VIJAYAKUMAR, K.P. (2002), "Kerala university Library; A SWOT analysis proposal for the marketing of information services", *KELPRO Bulletin, Vol.8* (1&2), 2002, pp.64-

LANCASTER, F.W. (1977), *The measurement and evaluation of library services*. Washington DC. Information Resources Press, 1977.

LANCASTER, F.W. (1978), *Guidelines for the evaluation of information systems and services*; Paris, Unesco Press, 1978. MISHAN, E.J. and QUAH, Easton (2007), *Cost-Benefit Analysis*, Edn. 5, Routledge, 2007.

OECD Glossary of Statistical Terms(2008), OECD

PARASURAMAN, A., BERRY, L.L., and ZEITHAML, V.A. (1991), "Refinement and Reassessment of the SERVQUAL Scale", *Journal of Retailing*, Vol.67 (4), 1991, Pp.420-450.

ROBERTS, S. A .(1985), Cost *management for library and information services*. Butterworth, 1985.

SURESH KUMAR, P.K. (2012), "University libraries in Kerala; A SWOT analysis for marketing *Library Philosophy and Practice (e-Journal), 2012*. University of Nebraska-Lincoln.

VERMA, R.K. (2002), "Measuring quality management level with reference to ISOI:9000 and TQM for special libraries in India", *Annals of Lib. & Inf. Studies* Vol. 49(4), 2002; pp.141-163.

Bibliography

ABBOTT, Christine (1994), *Performance measurement in library and information services*, London, ASLIB, 1994

AHMAD, Hilal (2016), *Integrated Library Management Systems; the Indian Scenario of Modern Library Automation,* New Delhi, Ess Ess Publications, 224 P.

ALBERT, William (2013), *Measuring the User Experience; Collecting, Analyzing, and Presenting* Usability Metrics (Interactive Technologies), Edn.2, Morgan Kaufan, 322 P.

AL-HAWAMDEH, Suliman, (2003), *Knowledge Management; Cultivating Knowledge Professionals*, Oxford, Chandos Publishing, 2003.

AMERICAN LIBRARY ASSOCIATION (1996), *Guide for training collection development librarians quoted in John Kennedy, Collection Management: A consise Introduction,* Wood head Publishing Limited 2006 (www.sciencedirct.com)

AMERICAN LIBRARY ASSOCIATION (2006), *Guidelines for the introduction of electronic information resources to users, prepared for the Reference and User Services Association of the ALA, (revised in 2006).*

APPLETON (Leo) (2017), *Libraries and Key Performance Indicators: A Frame work for Practitioners*, Chandos Publishing, 2017.

ASIAN DEVELOPMENT BANK (2013), *Cost-Benefit Analysis for Development; A Practical Guide*, Institutional Document, January 2013.

ATHERTON, Pauline. *Handbook of information systems and services*, Paris, UNESCO, 1977.

ATHAWALE, Swapna (2014), *Scientific Management in Libraries; A Method to Grow and Survive in this Competitive Era,* Published by Maltesh Moteberems, Itanagar, Arunachal Pradesh.

BALLABH, Anand (2000), *Modern Scientific Management of Libraries*, New Delhi, Rajat, 245 P.

AUGUSTINE, C.A. (1993), *Library and Information System (KAULIS)*, Thrissur, Kerala Agricultural University, 28 P.

AUGUSTINE, C.A. (2000), *"Digital Revolution Syndrome and Libraries"* in Devarajan, G. (Ed), New Challenges in Librarianship, New Delhi, Ess Ess Publications, Pp.12-28.

AUGUSTINE, C.A. (2004), *"Professional Education for Digital Libraraianship"* in Jalaja, V, et al (Eds), Organization, Processing and Use of Information in the Digital Era (Prof, M. Parameswaran Feschrift), New Delhi, Ess Ess Publications, Pp. 34-47.

AUGUSTINE, C.A. (2015), *"Social Informatics in LIS Research"* National Library Week 2015 KELPRO Souvenir, Trivandrum, Kerala University, Pp.25-28.

BALASUBRAMANIAN, P.(2021), *Digital Libraries*, New Delhi, Ess Ess Publications,

BALASUBRAMANIAN, P. and YOHANNAN, Sherin (2021), *Library Automation and Digitization*, New Delhi, Ess Publicatios

BARNARD, Susan B. (1997), *'Total Quality Management'* in Encyclopaedia of Library and Information Science, (ed. By Allen Kent & Harold Lancour) 1997 Vol. 61: pp. 311-25, Marcel Dekker, 1997.

BAVAKUTTY, M. and ABDUL MAJEED, K.C. (2005), *Methods for measuring quality of libraries* New Delhi, Ess Ess Publications, 2005.

BAXTER, Kathy and COURAGE, Catherine (2005), *Understanding Your Uses: A Practical Guide to User Requirements, Methods, Tools and Techniques (Interactive Technologies)*, Morgan Kaufman, 704 P.

BELLEW, Richard K. ***Finding Out About***; *A Cognitive Perspective on Search EngineTechnology and the WWW.* ,Cambridge University Press.

BERNAL, J.D. et al (1948) *"The Royal Society Scientific Information Conference"* ***Nature*** 162;279-286, (1948).

BHATTACHARYYA, G. (1982) *"Some of the basic principles of Library Science based on the Five Laws of Library/Science"* ***Library Science with a Slant to Documentation,*** 1982. DRTC, Bangalore.

BHARADWAJ, H.C. (1979), *Aspects of Ancient Indian Technology; A Research Based on Scientific Method,* Motilal Banarasidas, 226 P.

BINDHU P. NAIR (2008), *'User's perspective on Total Quality Management in Kerala University Library: an analytical study'*, ***KELPRO Bulletin*** 12(2), Dec. 2008, Pp.74-94.

BOEKHORST, Peter te (1995), *"Measuring Quality: the IFLA Guidelines for Performance Measurement in Academic Libraries"* **IFLA Journal** Vol.21(4),1995, Pp.278-281.

BONNE, George S. (1971)."*Chapter 2 Information Sources*" shodhganga,inflibnet,ac,in downloaded on 18/08/2020

BRYSON, Jo.(1997), *Managing information services; an integrated approach,* Hampshire, Gower, 1997.

BRYSON, Joe (1998), *Effective Library and Information Centre Management,* Routeledge, P. 8.s

BURKE, Mary A. (1999), *Organization of Multimedia Resources : Principles and Practice of Information Retreival,* England, Gower Publishing,

CHATTOPADHYAYA, Debiprasad (1996), *History of Scienee and Technology in Ancient India: the Beginnings,* with a foreword by Joseph Needham, Firkma KLM Private Limited.

CHAUBEY, Ajay Kumar (2016), *Transformation of Library Services in Electronic Era,* Studera Press

CHOWDHURI, G.G. (2004), *Introduction to Modern Information Retrieval,* Edn.2, London, Facet Publishing.

COHN, John M, et al. (2002), *Planning for Integrated Systems and Technologies; a how-to-do-it Manual for Librarians,* Edn.2,Revised by David Salter, London Facet Publishing,2002.

COLEMAN, Vicki, et. al.(1997) "*Toward a TQM paradigm: Using SERVQUAL to measure library service quality*". ***College and Research Libraries*** Vol.58(3),1997.

CONEY, Donald (1930). *'Scientific management and university libraries' in Schwenning, G.T. Management problems,* University of North Carolina, Carolina Press, 2017(originally published in 1930), pp.168-198.

CONEY, Donald (1952), *'Management in college and university libraries' Library Trends,* vol.1 July 1952 pp.83-94.

COOK, C. & HEATH, F.(2001), "*User's perceptions of library service quality: A LibQUAL qualitative study*", ***Library Trends*** Vol. 49 (4), 2001,:pp.548-584.

COOKE, Alison (2001), *A Guide to Finding Quality Informat;ion on the Internet; Selection and Evaluation Strategies, Edn.2,* London, Library Association.

CORRAL, Sheilla (2000). *Strategic management of information services; a planning handbook,* Taylor & Francis, 2000.

CORRALL, Sheila and BREWERTON, Antony (1999), *The new professional's handbook; your guide to information services.* London, Library Association, 1999.

CRUMPTON, Michael A. (2015), *Strategic Human Resources Planning for Academic Libraries,* Chandos Publishing 110 P.

CSIR – NISTADS (2014), India: *Science and Technology, ed by National Institute of Science, Technology and Development Studies*, Cambridge.CUSHING, Frank Hamilton (1896) Zuni Folk Tales, Good Press publishers, 1896

De SAEZ, Eileen Elliot (2002), *Marketing Concepts for Libraries and Information Services*, Edn.2, London, Facet Publishing.

DEMING, W. Edwards (1982),. *Out of the Crisis, MIT Centre for Advanced Engineering Study*,1982.

DEMING, W. Edwards (1986) *Out of the Crisis: Quality, Productivity and Competitive Position,* Cambridge university Press,1986.

DEMING, W. Edwards,(1993*) The New Economics for Industry, Government and Education,* Boston, Ma, MIT Press,1993

DESS, Gregory B., et al. (2005), *Strategic management, edn.2,* New York, McGraw-Hill Irwin, 2005.

DEVARAJAN, G. (1995), *Library Information Users and Use Studies*, New Delhi, Beacon Books

DEVARAJAN, G. (Ed) (2005), *Library and Information Studies in the Digital Age* (Prof. K. A. Isaac Commemoration Volume), New Delhi, Ess Ess Publications,

DEVARAJAN, G. (Ed) (2019*), Encyclopaedia of Science Information,* New Delhi, Ess Ess Publications, , 412 P.

DHAMDHERA, Sangeeta, and LITHIKAR, Ramdas (2021), *Web Based Services: A Transforming Revolution in Modern Libraries,* New Delhi, Ess Ess Publications.

DHIMAN, Anil K and RANI, Yashoda (2005),, Learn *Library management,* (New Delhi, Ess. Ess. Publns, 2005.

DROTT, M. Carl and GRIFFITH, Belever C. (1978), "An Empirical View of Bradford's Law and the Scattering of Scientific Literature", ***Journal of American Society for Information Science and Technology (JASIST)*** Vol;. 29 (5) Pp.238-246.

DRUCKER, Peter (1973), *Management: tasks, responsibilities, practices,* Heinemann, 1973

DRUCKER, Peter F. (2001), *The Essential Drucker: In one Content the Best of Sixty Years of Peter Drucker's Esdsential Writings on Management;* Harper Business, 368 P. P.),

DRUCKER, Peter F. (2006), *The Practice of Management*, Harper Business, P.416.

DRUCKER, Peter F. (2008), *Management, Revised edition*, Harper Business, 608 P.EVANS, E.G. Management techniques for libraries, 1976

EZEANI, Chinwe Nwogo and IGWESI, Uzoamaka (2012), *"Using social media for dynamic library service delivery; the Nigerian experience" Library philosophy and practice (e-journal) 2012 paper no. 814* .http:// digitalcommons.unl.edu/libphilprac/814

FAYOL, Henri(1916), *General and industrial administration, (French original),* Paris, H. Dumond, 1916,(and English translation in 1949).

FORD, n. (2015), *Introduction to Information Behaviour,* London, Facet Publishing

GARFIELD, Eugene (1964), *The Science Citation Index,* Clarivate Analytics

GARFIELD, Eugene (1955) *"Citation Indexes for Science; A New Dimension in Documentation through Association of Ideas", **Science*** 122 (3159), PP.108-11.

GINES, de Rus (201o), *Introduction to Cost-Benefit Analysis: Looking for Reasonable Short Cuts,* Edward Edgar

GLADAMOSI, B.O. (2012*), "Emerging challenges to effective library automation and an e-library; the case of Emanuel Alayande College of Education, Oyo, Nigeria"* Library Philosophy and Practice (e-journal), 2012; paper no.807.

GLUCK, F.W., KAUFMAN, S & WALLECK, A.S.(1982), *'The four phases of strategic management', **Journal of Business Strategy,*** 2(3), 1982 pp.9-21.

GOODMAN, Elizabeth (2012), *Observing the User Experience: A Practical Guide to User Research, Edn.2,* Morgan Kaufman, 601 P.:

GOODSTEIN, L.D., NOLAN, T.M. & PFEIFFER, J.W. (1992), *Applied strategic planning; a comprehensive guide,* San Diego, CA Pfeiffer & Co, 1992.

GREGORY, Vicki L. (2019), *Collection Development and Management for 21st Century Library Collections; An Introduction,* Chicago, ALA Neal-Schuman, 264 P.

GREGORY, Vicki L.(2011) *Collection development and management for 21st century collections: an introduction,* London, Neal-Schuman Publishers, 2011.

GULICK, L.H. (1937) *: "Notes on the Theory of Organization" in L. Gulick & L. Urwick (eds), Papers on the Science of Administration,* New York, Institute of Public Administration, Pp3-45.

GUPTA, Sangita (2016), *Manpower Needs of Automated Liibraries,* New Delhi, Ess Ess Publications,

HIAM, Alexander (1992),. *Closing the Quality Gap; Lessons from America's Leading Companies,* Prentice Hall, Inc. 1992.

HORSTMAN, Mark (2016), *The Effective Manager,* Wiley 209 P.

HOWARD, Paul (1940), *'The functions of library management,* Library

Quarterly vol.10, July 1940 pp.313-349.

HUMPHREY, Albert (2005), *"SWOT Analysis for Management Consulting"* ***SRI Alumni Newsletter***, Stanford Research Institute International.

IGNOU (1989), *Library Management, Course BLS-2*, New Delhi, Indira Gandhi National Open University, P.6.

IFLA (2012), *Key Issues for e-resources collection development: a guide for libraries*, ed. by Sharon Johnson, et al. (Aug 2012)

INDIA, RESEARCH REFERENCE AND TRAINING DIVISOIN (2111), India 2011, A Reference Annual. Edn.55 New Delhi, Publications Division, 2011.

JABLONSKI, Joseph R.(1992), *Implementing TQM Competing in the Nineties Through Total Quality Management Edn.* 2. Technical Management Consortium, Inc. 1992.pp.64—76.

JAGGI, O.P. (1984), *Impact of Science and Technology in Modern India*, Atma Ram & Sons, 202 P

JAIN, Abhinandan K. et al Eds.(1999), *Marketing Information Products and Services; A Primer for Librarians and information Professionals*, New Delhi, IDRC & Tata McGraw-Hill,

JOHNSON, Peggy (2004), *Fundamentals of Collection Development and Management*, Chicago, American Library Association,2004 342 p.

JOHNSON, Peggy (2018), *Fundamentals of Collection Development and Management*, Edn. 4, ALA, 632 P.

JORDAN, Peter and JONES, Noragh (1987), *Staff management in library and information work*, edn. 3. England, Gower Publishing Company, 1987.

JURAN, Joseph M. (1974), *Quality Control Handbook*, New York, MacGraw-Hill

KRISHNA, C.Murali (2007), *Manpower Planning in University Libraries*, New Delhi Ess Ess Publications, 246 P.

LAHIRI, Abhijit, et al. (1998) *'National Information System for Science and Technology (NISSAT*) in Neelameghan, and Prasad(1998), op cit. Ch.14, pp.221-246.

LALI, S.L. and VIJAYAKUMAR, K.P. (2002), *"Kerala university Library; A SWOT analysis proposal for the marketing of information services"*, ***KELPRO Bulletin***, Vol.8 (1&2), 2002, pp.64-

MASON, Merilyn Gell (1999), *Strategic management for today's libraries*, ALA, 1999.

LANCASTER, F.W. (1968), Information Retrieval Systems; Characteristics, Testing and Evaluation , N.Y. Wiley.

LANCASTER, F.W. (1977), *The measurement and evaluation of library services.*

Washington DC. Information Resources Press, 1977.

LANCASTER, F.W. (1978), *Guidelines for the evaluation of information systems and services;* Paris, Unesco Press, 1978.

LEE, Stuart D. (2001), *Digital Imaging; A Practical Handbook*, London, Library Association

LEE, Stuart D. (2002), *Buildjng An Electronic Resource Collection; A Practical Guide* , London, Library Association.,

MATARAZZO, James M and CONNOLLY, Suzanna D. ((1999), *Knowledge and Special Libraries*, Boston, Butterworth-Heineman

MATHEWS, Joseph R.(2005), *Strategic planning and management for library managers*, Greenwood, USA, 2005.

MATHEWS, Joseph R. (2017), *The Evaluation and Measurment of Library Services*, Edn.2, Libraries Unlimited Inc.

MENZEL, Herbert (1964) *"The Information Needs of Current Scientific Research"* ***The Library Quarterly; Information, Community, Policy***, Vol.34 (1), Jan 1964 pp 4-19.

MISHAN, E.J. and QUAH, Easton (2007), *Cost-Benefit Analysis*, Edn. 5, Routledge, 2007.

MISHRA, C.S. (CIM, Patna) (2008), *Social networking technologies in digital environment: its possible implications on libraries,* E-LIS 2008 . Eprints.rclis.org/16844/1/Social%20networking%20Library.pdf

MORAN, Barbara (2017), *Library and Information Centre Management*, 9th edn, Libraries Unlimited, P. 548

NARCHAND, Donald A and HORTON,Jr.,Forest W.(1986), *Infotrends; Profiting from Your Information Resources,* New York, J:ohn Wiley

NATO ADVANCED STUDY INSTITUTE (1977), *Evaluation and Scientific Management of Libraries and Information Centres; Proceedings,* Nederlands, Leyden, Nordhoff.

NEELAMEGHAN, A. and PRASAD, K.N. Eds. (1998), *Information systems, networks and services: developments and trends 2 vols*. Bangalore, Institute of Information Studies,1998.

NYSTROM, Viveka and SJOGREN. Linnea (2012), *An Evaluation of the Benefits and Value of Libraries,* Chandos Publishing, 200 P.

PANTRY, Sheila and GRIFFITH, Peter (1995), *Becoming A Successful Interpreneur: A Practical Guide To Creating An Innovative Information Service,* London, Library Association.

PARASURAMAN, A., BERRY, L.L., and ZEITHAML, V.A. (1991), *"Refinement and Reassessment of the SERVQUAL Scale"*, ***Journal of Retailing,*** Vol.67 (4), 1991, Pp.420-450.

PATENT SYSTEM OF U.S.."(www..uspto.gov/).

PEARSON, Karl, (1911), *Grammar of Science*. Edn.3 (Originally published in 1892), Adam & Charles Black, 1911.

PENNA. Carlo Victor (1970), *The Planning of Libraries and Documentation Services, Edn 2,* Revised and enlarged by P.A. Sewell and Herrnan Liebaers, Unesco, 1970 158 P.

POLL, Roswitha and BOEEKHORST, Peter te ,Eds. (2007), *Measuri;ng Quality: Performance Measurement in Libraries,* 2nd revised edn, (First edn 1996), IFLA Publications, 127, Munich, K G Saur.

PRICE, Larry R, (2016), *Psychometric Methods: Theory into Practice,* The Guilford Press, New York, 2017.

PUGH, Lyndon (2000),*Change management in information services,* Hampshire, Gower, 2000.

RAJARAM, Kalpana (Ed), (2012), Developments *in Science and Technology,* Spectrum Books, (P) Ltd, , 855 p.

RAMAKRISHNAN, M.N. (2000), "*Professional Libaraianship in Kerala; A Critical Study by SWOT Analysis*" in Devarajan, G (Ed), New Challenges in Librarianship, New Delhi, Ess Ess Publications, Pp1-11.

RANGANATHAN, S.R. (1957), *Five Laws of Library Science*, Edn. 2 Bombay, Asia Publishing House, 1957.

RANGANATHAN, S.R. (1959*): Library Administration,* Edn.2, Bombay, Asia Publishing House.

RANGANATHAN, S.R.(1961), *Reference Service,* Edn.2, Bombay, Asia Publishing House, 1961.

RANGANATHAN, S.R. (1988), *The Five Laws of Library Science*, Bangalore, Sarada Ranganathan Endowment For Library Science, 1988.

RIGGS,(1992), "*TQM quality improvement in new clothes*", ***College & Research Libraries*** 53(6), 1992 pp.481-482

ROBERTS, S. A .(1985), *Cost management for library and information services.* Butterworth, 1985.

ROBERTS, Harry V. and Bernard F.(1993), Sergesketter. *Quality is Personal: A Foundation for Total Quality Management.* The Free Press, 1993.

ROBIINSON, Bruce Murray (1996), *Total Quality Management in Education: the empowerment of a school community,* Lincoln, University of Nebraska.

ROPTHAERMEL, Frank T. (2016), *Strategic Management*, Edn.3, McGraw-Hill Education, 208 P.

SACHDEVA, Iqbal S. (2009), *Public relations; principles and practices*, New

Delhi, Oxford University Press, 2009.

SAHU, Hemant Kumar, et al. (ICCAA, Pune) (2010), *New innovative library services: moving with Web* 2.0/ Library 2.0 technology ; a case study, LISA VI, Feb 14-17,2010.

SALTON, G. and McGILL, M. (1983), *Introduction to Modern Information Retrieval,* New York, McGraw-Hill.

SARKAR, D. (1998), *The Manager's Handbook for Total Quality Management,* Beacon Books, 1998.

SATPATHI, Kishor Chandra and KRISHNAMATHI SINGHA, Eds. (2017), *Emerging Trends and Human Resources Management in Library and Information Centre,* New Delhi, Shankar's Book Agency.

SEETHARAMA, S.(1990), *Guidelines for planning of libraries and information centres,* Calcutta, IASLIC, 1990

SHARMA , C.K. and SINGH, Kiran (2005), *Library Management,* 2 Volumes, Atlatntic Publishers & Distributors, 272+264 P.

SHAW, Ralph R. (1947), *'Scientific management in the library'* ***Wilson Library Bulletin,*** Vol 21, January 1947 pp.349-352.

SHAW, Ralph R.(1954), *'Introduction', Library Trends,* Vol. 2 (3); January 1954.pp

SHAW, Ralph R. (1956), *Pilot Study on the Use of Scientific Literature by Scientists,* Department of Agriculture, National Science Foundation, U.S.

SHERA, Jessy H. (1972) *Foundations for Education for Librarianship,* Becker & Hayes,1972.

SIATRI, R. (1999), *"The Evolution of User Studies"* , ***LIBRI*** P.132-141.

SINGH, Gurudev (2013), *Information Sources, Services and Systems,* PHI Learning, 517 P.

SKYRMA, David J. (2002), *Capitalizing On Knowledge; From e-business To k-business.* Oxford, Butterworth Heineman,.

SPILLER, David. *Providing materials for library users.* London, Library Association, 2000.

SRIDHAR, M .S. *Problems of Collection Development in Special Libraries,* New Delhi, Concept Publications, 1992..

SRIVASTAVAN, B.K. and NARASIMHAN, M.A. (2003), *Science and Technology in India Through the Ages,* Melkota, Academy of Sanskrit Research.

STEIN, M. Kyrillidou and DAVIS, D. (Eds) (2002), *Proceedings of the Fourth Northumbrian International Conference on Performance Measurement in Libraries and Information Services; Meaningful Measures for Emerging*

Realities, Washington DC, Association of "Research Librariies, 2002

SURAWEERA, S.W.(2010)," *Value of social networking in libraries and information organization in Asia and Oceania" in World Library and Information Congress:* 76th IFLA General Conference and Assembly, 10-15 August 2010, Gothenberg, Sweden

SURESH, J.K. and MAHESH, Kavi (2006), *Ten Steps to Maturity In Knowledge Management; Lessons In Economy*. Oxford, Chandos Publishing,

SURESH KUMAR, P.K. (2012), "University libraries in Kerala; *A SWOT analysis for marketing Library Philosophy and Practice (e-Journal),* 2012. University of Nebraska-Lincoln.

THAKURIA, Pranjit Kumar ((2007),. *'Concept of Quality in Library Services; an overview' in 5th Convention Planner 2007* Guahati University, Dec.7-8, 2007. Pp. 412-

TAYLOR, Frederick Winslow (1909/1911), *The Principles of Scientific Management*, Harper & Brothers Publishers 1919.

UNESCO (1987), International Reader in the Management of Library, Information and Archive Services. 684P.

VARSHNEY, Anamika (2011) *Sources of Information LIS BD Network, Library & Information Science* Academic Blog www.lisbdnet.com downloaded on 16/08/2020

VERMA. R.K.(2002), *'Measuring quality management level with reference to ISO 9000 and TQM for Special Libraries in India'*, ***Annals of Library & Information Studies***, 49(4), 2002 Pp.141-63.

VICKERY, Brian and VICKERY, Alina (1987), *Information Science in Theory and Practice*, London, Butterworth.

WELLS, Denise Lindsey (1998), *Strategic management for senior leaders: a handbook for implementation,* U.S. Dept of Navy Total Quality Leadership Office Publication No. 94-02,1998, 2015.

WILSON, Alexander (1978). *Planning approach to library management,* London, Library Association, 1978.

WILSON, Louis R. (1938). *The Geography of Reading; a study of the distribution and status of libraries in the United States,* Chicago, University of Chicago Press, 1938.

WILSON-DAVIS, K. (1976) "*CRUS – Its Functions and Aims*", ***Library Review***, 1 May 1976